D0399078

GORDON B. HINCKLEY

STAND A LITTLE TALLER

COUNSEL AND INSPIRATION
FOR EACH DAY OF THE YEAR

EAGLE
GATE
SALT LAKE CITY, UTAH

Visit us at www.deseretbook.com

Library of Congress Cataloging-in-Publication Data
  Hinckley, Gordon Bitner, 1910-
    Stand a little taller / Gordon B. Hinckley.
      p.   cm.
  ISBN 1-57008-767-9 (alk. paper)
  1. Christian life—Mormon authors.   I. Title.
BX8656.H565   2001
242—dc21   2001004016

Printed in the United States of America   42316-6911
Menomonee Falls, WI

10   9   8

Though our outward man perish, yet the inward man is renewed day by day.

—2 CORINTHIANS 4:16

PREFACE

President Gordon B. Hinckley has asked us all to "stand tall and live the gospel." He has, through example, shown us how this is possible and demonstrated the great good that members of The Church of Jesus Christ of Latter-day Saints can do throughout the world.

As you read this collection of thoughts and scripture, we hope that you will discover the truth in each piece of wisdom and advice from our living prophet. We hope you will learn that a part of his faith resides in his desire for each member of the Church to be a light to the world by living the gospel and serving in the kingdom of God.

Above all, we hope that you will find in these pages the motivation and inspiration to follow the prophet, to make each day a little better than the one before, and to "stand a little taller."

—The Publisher

JANUARY

If ye shall press forward, feasting upon the word of Christ, and endure to the end, behold, thus saith the Father: Ye shall have eternal life.

—2 NEPHI 31:20

STAND A LITTLE TALLER

Watch ye, stand fast in the faith,
quit you like men, be strong.
—1 CORINTHIANS 16:13

The time has come for us to stand a little taller, to lift our eyes and stretch our minds to a greater comprehension and understanding of the grand millennial mission of this The Church of Jesus Christ of Latter-day Saints. This is a season to be strong. It is a time to move forward without hesitation, knowing well the meaning, the breadth, and the importance of our mission. It is a time to do what is right regardless of the consequences that might follow. We have nothing to fear. God is at the helm. He will overrule for the good of the work.

A Sense of Peace

*Let us therefore follow after the things which
make for peace, and things wherewith
one may edify another.*

—ROMANS 14:19

All of us have to deal with death at one time or another, but to have in one's heart a solid conviction concerning the reality of eternal life is to bring a sense of peace in an hour of tragedy and loss that can come from no other source under the heavens.

BE A LITTLE BETTER

Be of good comfort, be of one mind, live in peace;
and the God of love and peace shall be with you.

—2 CORINTHIANS 13:11

We are all in this together, all of us, and we have a great work to do.

Every teacher can be a better teacher than he or she is today.

Every officer can be a better officer than he or she is today.

Every father can be a better father.

Every mother can be a better mother.

Every husband can be a better husband, every wife a better wife, every child a better child.

We are on the road that leads to immortality and eternal life and today is a part of it. Let us never forget it.

HIS WORK AND HIS GLORY

Behold, are ye stripped of pride? I say unto you,
if ye are not ye are not prepared to meet God.
Behold ye must prepare quickly; for the
kingdom of heaven is soon at hand,
and such an one hath not eternal life.

—ALMA 5:28

Adulation is poison. It is so very important that you do not let praise and adulation go to your head. Never lose sight of the fact that the Lord put you where you are according to His design, which you don't fully understand. Acknowledge the Lord for whatever good you can accomplish and give Him the credit and the glory.

THE TEMPLE AND IMMORTALITY

Herein is glory and honor,
and immortality and eternal life.

—DOCTRINE AND COVENANTS 128:12

The temple is concerned with things of immortality. It is a bridge between this life and the next. All of the ordinances that take place in the house of the Lord are expressions of our belief in the immortality of the human soul.

FAITH OVERCOMES

*If ye have faith as a grain of mustard seed, ye shall
say unto this mountain, Remove hence to yonder
place; and it shall remove; and nothing shall
be impossible unto you.*

—MATTHEW 17:20

There is no obstacle too great, no challenge too
difficult, if we have faith.

THE POWER OF PRAYER

Behold, I stand at the door, and knock: if any man hear my voice, and open the door, I will come in to him, and will sup with him, and he with me.

—REVELATION 3:20

The trouble with most of our prayers is that we give them as if we were picking up the telephone and ordering groceries—we place our order and hang up. We need to meditate, contemplate, think of what we are praying about and for and then speak to the Lord as one man speaketh to another. "Come now, and let us reason together, saith the Lord" (Isaiah 1:18). That is the invitation. Believe in the power of prayer—it is real, it is wonderful, it is tremendous.

HEALING POWER

Is any sick among you? let him call for the elders of the church; and let them pray over him, anointing him with oil in the name of the Lord.

—JAMES 5:14

The power to heal the sick is still among us. It is the power of the priesthood of God. It is the authority held by the elders of this Church.

We are indebted to the dedicated men and women of science and medicine who have conquered so much of disease, who have stayed the hand of death. I cannot say enough of gratitude for them. Yet they are the first to admit the limitations of their knowledge and skills in dealing with many matters of life and death. The mighty Creator of the heavens and the earth has given to His servants a divine power that sometimes transcends all the power and knowledge of mankind.

THREE THINGS ALL CONVERTS NEED

Go ye therefore, and teach all nations,
baptizing them in the name of the Father,
and of the Son, and of the Holy Ghost.

—MATTHEW 28:19

With the ever-increasing number of converts, we must make an increasingly substantial effort to assist them as they find their way. Every one of them needs three things: a friend, a responsibility, and nourishing with the "good word of God" (Moroni 6:4). It is our duty and opportunity to provide these things.

SEEK THE LORD IN PRAYER

Whatsoever ye shall ask the Father in my name,
which is right, believing that ye shall receive,
behold it shall be given unto you.

—3 NEPHI 18:20

Call upon the Lord. He has extended the invitation, and He will answer. Believe in prayer and the power of prayer. Pray to the Lord with the expectation of answers.

FAMILY RELATIONSHIPS

*See that ye love one another, . . . learn to impart
one to another as the gospel requires.*

—DOCTRINE AND COVENANTS 88:123

God has brought us together as families to bring
to pass His eternal purposes. We are part of this
plan in this marriage relationship. Let us love and
respect and honor one another. We can do it, and
we will be the better for it.

DAILY CHOICES

By small and simple things are
great things brought to pass.

—ALMA 37:6

The course of our lives is seldom determined by great, life-altering decisions. Our direction is often set by the small, day-to-day choices that chart the track on which we run. This is the substance of our lives—making choices.

THE SACRAMENTAL ORDINANCE

Whoso eateth my flesh, and drinketh my blood,
hath eternal life; and I will raise him up in
the resurrection of the just at the last day.

—JST, JOHN 6:54

The sacrament and the partaking of these emblems is the very heart of our Sabbath worship. It includes a renewal of covenants with God. It carries with it a promise of His Holy Spirit to be with us. As we partake of the sacrament we can all stand on a level plane before the Lord. Each is accountable for what he does as he renews his covenants with the Lord in that magnificent and beautiful and simple ordinance of the gospel which carries with it such tremendous meaning.

A RIGHTEOUS BATTLE

*Put on the whole armour of God, that ye may be
able to stand against the wiles of the devil. For
we wrestle not against flesh and blood, but
against principalities, against powers,
against the rulers of the darkness of
this world, against spiritual
wickedness in high places.*

—EPHESIANS 6:11–12

We are involved in an intense battle. It is a battle
between right and wrong, between truth and error,
between the design of the Almighty on the one
hand and that of Lucifer on the other. For that reason, we desperately need moral men and women
who stand on principle, to be involved in the polit-
ical process. Otherwise, we abdicate power to those
whose designs are almost entirely selfish.

DO WHAT IS RIGHT

Be faithful and diligent in keeping the
commandments of God, and I will encircle
thee in the arms of my love.

—DOCTRINE AND COVENANTS 6:20

Be true to your convictions. You know what is right, and you know what is wrong. You know when you are doing the proper thing. You know when you are giving strength to the right cause. Be loyal. Be faithful. Be true.

THE VALUE OF GOOD BOOKS

Seek ye out of the best books
words of wisdom.

–DOCTRINE AND COVENANTS 88:118

Good books are as friends, willing to give to us if we are willing to make a little effort.

MEEK IN SPIRIT

Blessed are the meek:
for they shall inherit the earth.

—MATTHEW 5:5

The meek and the humble are those who are teachable. They are willing to learn. They are willing to listen to the whisperings of the still, small voice for guidance in their lives. They place the wisdom of the Lord above their own wisdom.

THE EVILS OF SELFISHNESS

All we like sheep have gone astray; we have turned
every one to his own way; and the Lord hath
laid on him the iniquity of us all.

—ISAIAH 53:6

Selfishness is the basis of our troubles—a vicious
preoccupation with our own comforts and with
the satisfaction of our own appetites.

RIGHTEOUS CONVICTIONS

*It has been made known unto you, by the testimony
of his word, that he cannot walk in crooked paths;
neither doth he vary from that which he hath
said; neither hath he a shadow of turning
from the right to the left, or from that which
is right to that which is wrong; therefore,
his course is one eternal round.*

—ALMA 7:20

In this world so filled with problems, so constantly threatened by dark and evil challenges, you can and must rise above mediocrity, above indifference. You can become involved and speak with a strong voice for that which is right.

A RIGHTEOUS PEOPLE

O come, let us worship and bow down:
let us kneel before the Lord our maker.

—PSALM 95:6

Let the pulpits of all the churches ring with righteousness. Let people everywhere bow in reverence before the Almighty who is our one true strength. Let us look inward and adjust our priorities and standards. Let us look outward in the spirit of the Golden Rule.

GROWING IN LIGHT

That which is of God is light; and he that receiveth
light, and continueth in God, receiveth more
light; and that light groweth brighter
and brighter until the perfect day

—DOCTRINE AND COVENANTS 50:24

What a remarkable plan—a light that grows "brighter and brighter until the perfect day." It speaks of growth, of development, of the march that leads toward godhood. What a profound challenge! We must go on growing. We must continually learn. It is a divinely given mandate that we go on adding to our knowledge.

RETURN GOOD FOR EVIL

Blessed are ye, when men shall revile you, and persecute you, and shall say all manner of evil against you falsely, for my sake

—MATTHEW 5:11

Draw comfort from the words of the Master when we as a church are spoken of by those whose lives are torn with hate. They lash out at one thing and another. They manufacture and spread vile falsehoods behind which there is not a shred of truth. There is nothing new about this. But we shall go forward, returning good for evil, being helpful and kind and generous.

COURAGEOUS CONVICTIONS

For I am not ashamed of the gospel of Christ:
for it is the power of God unto salvation
to every one that believeth.

—ROMANS 1:16

Paul wrote to Timothy: "God hath not given us the spirit of fear; but of power, and of love, and of a sound mind. Be not thou therefore ashamed of the testimony of our Lord" (2 Timothy 1:7–8). I would that every member of this Church would put those words where you might see them every morning as you begin your day. They will give you courage to speak up, they will give you the faith to try, they will strengthen your conviction of the Lord Jesus Christ.

THE SELFLESSNESS OF TEMPLE WORK

*Now therefore ye are no more strangers and
foreigners, but fellowcitizens with the saints,
and of the household of God; And are built
upon the foundation of the apostles and
prophets, Jesus Christ himself being the
chief corner stone; In whom all the
building fitly framed together groweth
unto an holy temple in the Lord.*

—EPHESIANS 2:19–21

Vicarious temple work for the dead more nearly
approaches the vicarious sacrifice of the Savior
Himself than any other work of which I know. No
one comes with any expectation of thanks for the
work which he or she does. It is given with love,
without hope of compensation, or repayment.
What a glorious principle!

GOOD FOR SOMETHING

*For I remember the word of God which saith by
their works ye shall know them; for if their
works be good, then they are good also.*

—MORONI 7:5

You are good. But it is not enough just to be
good. You must be good for something. You must
contribute good to the world. The world must be a
better place for your presence. And the good that
is in you must be spread to others.

LESSONS OF FAMILY

*Pray in your families . . . that your wives
and your children may be blessed.*

—3 NEPHI 18:21

It is within families that truth is best learned, integrity is cultivated, self-discipline is instilled, and love is nurtured.

THE SABBATH

Remember the sabbath day, to keep it holy.

—EXODUS 20:8

Keep the Sabbath holy," saith the Lord to all people and particularly to this people. On the first Sabbath in the Salt Lake Valley, Brigham Young said, "We will not work on Sunday, for those who do will lose five times as much as they gain." I believe God will honor and bless and magnify and be quick to help those who try to keep His commandments. The commandment on the Sabbath Day is the longest of the Ten Commandments. The Lord was very specific about it, very detailed about it. I can't help but believe that the merchants would not be open on Sunday if we did not patronize their stores. Therefore, that responsibility rests upon our shoulders. I hope you will not shop on Sunday.

THE POWER OF GOODNESS

Charge them that are rich in this world, that they
be not highminded, nor trust in uncertain riches,
but in the living God, who giveth us richly all
things to enjoy; That they do good, that they
be rich in good works, ready to distribute,
willing to communicate.

—1 TIMOTHY 6:17–18

Great is your power for good. Marvelous are your talents and devotion. Tremendous is your faith and your love for the Lord, for His work, and for His sons and daughters. Continue to live the gospel. Magnify it before all of your associates. Your good works will carry more weight than any words you might speak.

THE MIRACLE OF CONVERSION

And according to his faith there was a
mighty change wrought in his heart.

—ALMA 5:12

There is no miracle like the miracle of conversion. It is the great process by which those with responsive hearts listen to the teachings and testimonies of missionaries and change their lives, leaving the past behind them, and moving forward into a new life. There is no miracle quite like it in all the world.

BUILDING THE KINGDOM

Therefore now let your hands be strengthened,
and be ye valiant.

—2 SAMUEL 2:7

This work requires sacrifice, it requires effort, it requires courage to speak out and faith to try.

LIVING THE GOSPEL

See that ye take care of these sacred things,
yea, see that ye look to God and live.

—ALMA 37:47

Let us live the gospel. Let it shine in our lives. Let it shine in our faces. Let it come through our actions. Live the gospel. Look to God and live.

FEBRUARY

*There is no fear in
love; but perfect love
casteth out fear.*

—1 JOHN 4:18

FOLLOWING THE EXAMPLE OF CHRIST

Christ also suffered for us, leaving us an example,
that ye should follow his steps.

—1 PETER 2:21

We must not, we cannot sink to the evils of the world—to selfishness and sin, to hate and envy and backbiting, to the "mean and beggarly" elements of life. You and I must walk on a higher plane. It may not be easy, but we can do it. Our great example is the Son of God whom we wish to follow.

LIFE IN CHRIST

If any man will come after me, let him deny himself, and take up his cross daily, and follow me.

—LUKE 9:23

The Lord declared: "He that findeth his life shall lose it: and he that loseth his life for my sake shall find it" (Matthew 10:39). These words have something more than a cold theological meaning. They are a statement of a law of life—that as we lose ourselves in a great cause we find ourselves—and there is no greater cause than that of the Master.

SHARED BURDENS

*And now, as ye are desirous to come into the fold of
God, and to be called his people, and are willing to
bear one another's burdens, that they may be light;
. . . and to stand as witnesses of God at all times
and in all things, and in all places that ye may be
in, even until death, that ye may be redeemed of
God, and be numbered with those of the first resurrection, that ye may have eternal life.*

—MOSIAH 18:8–9

Look above your trials. Try to forget your own
pain as you work to alleviate the pain of others.
Mingle together with your brothers and sisters in
the gospel. We need others to talk with and to
share our feelings and faith. Cultivate friends.
Begin by being a good friend to others. Share your
burdens with the Lord.

YOUR BEST SELF

Do all things . . . that ye may be blameless and
harmless, the sons of God, without rebuke, in the
midst of a crooked and perverse nation, among
whom ye shine as lights in the world.

—PHILIPPIANS 2:14–15

Keep faith with the best that is in you. Your own constant self-improvement will become as a polar star to those with whom you associate. They will remember longer what they saw in you than what they heard from you. Your attitude, your point of view can make such a tremendous difference.

THE PAST, PRESENT, AND FUTURE

Verily I say, men should be anxiously engaged in a good cause, and do many things of their own free will, and bring to pass much righteousness.

—DOCTRINE AND COVENANTS 58:27

How glorious is the past of this great cause. It is filled with heroism, courage, boldness, and faith. How wondrous is the present as we move forward to bless the lives of people wherever they will hearken to the message of the servants of the Lord. How magnificent will be the future as the Almighty rolls on His glorious work, touching for good all who will accept and live His gospel, and even reaching to the eternal blessing of His sons and daughters of all generations through the selfless work of those whose hearts are filled with love for the Redeemer of the world.

LIFE ETERNAL

And that same sociality which exists among us here
will exist among us there, only it will be
coupled with eternal glory, which
glory we do not now enjoy.
—DOCTRINE AND COVENANTS 130:2

I know as surely as anything in this world, that someday I shall die as to the life of this world. But I have an absolute certainty in my heart that I shall go on living and doing good and having the association of my beloved companion and my children.

ENRICH YOUR ENVIRONMENT

And do thou grant, Holy Father, that all those who
shall worship in this house may be taught words
of wisdom out of the best books, and that
they may seek learning even by study,
and also by faith, as thou hast said.

—DOCTRINE AND COVENANTS 109:14

A great man was once asked which one of all the books he had read had most affected his life. His response was that he could no more remember the books he had read than he could remember the meals he had eaten, but they had made him. All of us are the products of the elements to which we are exposed. We can give direction to those elements and thereby improve the result. Make every effort to enrich your environment with the reading of good books.

PROPHECY FULFILLED

What I the Lord have spoken, I have spoken, and I excuse not myself; and though the heavens and the earth pass away, my word shall not pass away, but shall all be fulfilled, whether by mine own voice or by the voice of my servants, it is the same.

—DOCTRINE AND COVENANTS 1:38

On a dark and winter day in 1849, in the old tabernacle, when the people were hungry and cold, Brigham Young said that the day would come when this would become the great highway of the nations and people from over the earth would visit us here. We are witnessing that day and the fulfillment of that remarkable prophecy.

TEMPLE PREPARATION

Yea, come unto Christ, and be perfected in him, and
deny yourselves of all ungodliness; and if ye shall
deny yourselves of all ungodliness, and love God
with all your might, mind and strength, then is
his grace sufficient for you, that by his grace
ye may be perfect in Christ; and if by the
grace of God ye are perfect in Christ, ye
can in nowise deny the power of God.

—MORONI 10:32

I plead with you, as one who loves you, to prepare yourselves to come to the house of the Lord. We have a large number of devoted and faithful Saints who go to the temple, but we have thousands and tens of thousands who do not go. To you, my brothers and sisters, to you whom I love so much, I make a plea to you to get your lives in order, to qualify for a temple recommend, to go to the house of the Lord.

DIVINE NATURE

*Put on therefore, as the elect of God, holy and
beloved, bowels of mercies, kindness, humbleness of
mind, meekness, longsuffering; Forbearing one
another, and forgiving one another, if any man
have a quarrel against any: even as Christ
forgave you, so also do ye.*

—COLOSSIANS 3:12–13

Each of us is a son or daughter of God, endowed
with something of his divine nature. Each is an
individual entitled to expression and cultivation of
individual talents and deserving of forbearance,
of patience, of understanding, of courtesy, of
thoughtful consideration.

MISSIONARY PREPARATION

*You must prepare yourselves by doing the things
which I have commanded you and required of you.*

—DOCTRINE AND COVENANTS 78:7

Young men, prepare for missionary service. Save money for that purpose. Save it in a secure way so that it will be available when you need it. Study a foreign language if you have opportunity to do so. Take advantage of every opportunity to enlarge your understanding of the gospel. Make the effort to participate in seminary and institute programs. The Lord's work needs the very best you are capable of providing. Now is the time to prepare for service. Keep yourselves clean as those worthy to represent the Lord before the world.

LOVE OVERCOMES

For God so loved the world, that he gave his only
begotten Son, that whosoever believeth in him
should not perish, but have everlasting life.

—JOHN 3:16

Love is the only force that can erase the differences between people—that can bridge chasms of bitterness.

THE ESSENCE OF LIFE

Wherefore, my beloved brethren, pray unto the Father with all the energy of heart, that ye may be filled with this love, which he hath bestowed upon all who are true followers of his Son, Jesus Christ; that ye may become the sons of God; that when he shall appear we shall be like him, for we shall see him as he is; that we may have this hope; that we may be purified even as he is pure.

—MORONI 7:48

Love is the very essence of life. It is the pot of gold at the end of the rainbow. Yet it is more than the end of the rainbow. Love is the security for which children weep, the yearning of youth, the adhesive that binds marriage, and the lubricant that prevents devastating friction in the home; it is the peace of old age, the sunlight of hope shining through death.

TRUE LOVE

Thou shalt live together in love.

—DOCTRINE AND COVENANTS 42:45

True love is not so much a matter of romance as it is a matter of anxious concern for the well-being of one's companion.

Rely on the Lord

*And by hearkening to observe all the words which
I, the Lord their God, shall speak unto them, they
shall never cease to prevail until the kingdoms
of the world are subdued under my feet,
and the earth is given unto the saints,
to possess it forever and ever.*

—DOCTRINE AND COVENANTS 103:7

The Lord has given you this glorious Church, His Church, to guide you and direct you, to give you opportunity for growth and experience, to teach you and lead you and encourage you, to make of you His chosen daughter or son, one upon whom He may look with love and with a desire to help. Of course there will be some problems along the way. There will be difficulties to overcome. But they will not last forever. He will not forsake you.

WALK IN OBEDIENCE

For you shall live by every word that proceedeth
forth from the mouth of God.

—DOCTRINE AND COVENANTS 84:44

The way of the gospel is a simple way. Some of the requirements may appear to you as elementary and unnecessary. Do not spurn them. Humble yourselves, and walk in obedience. I promise that the results that follow will be marvelous to behold and satisfying to experience.

A SPIRITUAL FEAST

And now, behold, I give unto you a commandment,
that when ye are assembled together ye shall
instruct and edify each other, that ye may
know how to act and direct my church,
how to act upon the points of my law and
commandments, which I have given.

—DOCTRINE AND COVENANTS 43:8

Every sacrament meeting ought to be a spiritual feast. It ought to be a time for meditation and introspection, a time for singing songs of praise to the Lord, a time for renewing one's covenant with Him and our Eternal Father, and a time for hearing the word of the Lord with reverence and appreciation.

STRENGTHEN FAITH AND TESTIMONY

But wilt thou know, O vain man,
that faith without works is dead?

—JAMES 2:20

Faith and testimony are like the muscles of my arm. If I use those muscles and nourish them, they grow stronger. If I put my arm in a sling, and leave it there, it becomes weak and ineffective, and so it is with testimony.

THE PRINCIPLE OF SACRIFICE

And to love him with all the heart, and with all the understanding, and with all the soul, and with all the strength, and to love his neighbour as himself, is more than all whole burnt offerings and sacrifices.

—MARK 12:33

Sacrifice is the very essence of religion; it is the keystone of happy home life, the basis for true friendship, the foundation of peaceful community living, of sound relations among people and nations. Without sacrifice there is no true worship of God.

TOLERANCE

Let every man esteem his
brother as himself

—DOCTRINE AND COVENANTS 38:24

We are taught as members of this Church to be
tolerant, to bring about good results, not to give in
on our doctrine, not to give in on our standards,
but to be tolerant in a way that will move forward
the cause of peace and righteousness and goodness
in the earth. May the Lord bless us to do so.

LOVE AT HOME

Cease to be idle; cease to be unclean; cease to find
fault one with another; ... And above all things,
clothe yourselves with the bond of charity, as with a
mantle, which is the bond of perfectness and peace.

—DOCTRINE AND COVENANTS 88:124–25

Imagine how our own families, let alone the world, would change if we vowed to keep faith with one another, strengthen one another, look for and accentuate the virtues in one another, and speak graciously concerning one another. Imagine the cumulative effect if we treated each other with respect and acceptance, if we willingly provided support. Such interactions practiced on a small scale would surely have a rippling effect throughout our homes and communities and, eventually, society at large.

CONTINUE IN GOODNESS

Therefore, blessed are ye if ye
continue in my goodness.

—DOCTRINE AND COVENANTS 86:11

Today will never come again. "Have I done any good in the world today? Have I helped anyone in need?"

A Noble Birthright

Walk worthy of God, who hath called you
unto his kingdom and glory.

—1 THESSALONIANS 2:12

This is a day of prophecy fulfilled . . . this great day in the history of this Church. This is the day which has been spoken of by those who have gone before us. Let us live worthy of our birthright.

WISDOM

Seek not for riches but for wisdom, and behold, the
mysteries of God shall be unfolded unto you,
and then shall you be made rich. Behold,
he that hath eternal life is rich.

—DOCTRINE AND COVENANTS 6:7

True wisdom cannot be obtained unless it is built on a foundation of true humility and gratitude.

A MATTER OF THE HEART

Verily I say unto you, Except ye be converted, and
become as little children, ye shall not enter
into the kingdom of heaven.

—MATTHEW 18:3

It is so important to see that we are all converted, that we have in our hearts a conviction concerning this great work. It is not a matter of the head only. It is a matter of the heart. It is being touched by the Holy Spirit until we know that this work is true, that Joseph Smith was verily a prophet of God, that God lives and that Jesus Christ lives and that they appeared to the boy Joseph Smith, that the Book of Mormon is true, that the priesthood is here with all of its gifts and blessings.

THE ESSENCE OF FAITH

*But behold, if ye will awake and arouse your
faculties, even to an experiment upon my words,
and exercise a particle of faith, yea, even if ye can
no more than desire to believe, let this desire work
in you, even until ye believe in a manner that ye
can give place for a portion of my words.*

—ALMA 32:27

Faith is the basis of testimony. Faith underlies loyalty to the Church. Faith represents sacrifice, gladly
given in moving forward the work of the Lord.

THE VALUE OF WORK

Work with your own hands.

—1 THESSALONIANS 4:11

I believe in the gospel of work. There is no substitute under the heavens for productive labor. It is the process by which dreams become reality. It is the process by which idle visions become dynamic achievements. We are all inherently lazy. We would rather play than work. We would rather loaf than work. A little play and a little loafing are good. But it is work that spells the difference in the life of a man or a woman. It is stretching our minds and utilizing the skills of our hands that lifts us from the stagnation of mediocrity.

AGENCY

For whatsoever a man soweth,
that shall he also reap.

—GALATIANS 6:7

Every generation that has ever walked the earth has faced challenges. But of all the challenges that have been faced in the past, the ones we have today, I believe, are most easily handled because they largely involve individual behavior decisions; decisions that can be made and followed when we exercise individual choice.

MARCH

And if ye do always remember me ye shall have my Spirit to be with you.

—3 NEPHI 18:7

ACCENTUATE THE POSITIVE

Men are, that they might have joy.

—2 NEPHI 2:25

I am asking that we stop seeking out the storms and enjoy more fully the sunlight. I am suggesting that as we go through life we "accentuate the positive." I am asking that we look a little deeper for the good, that we still voices of insult and sarcasm, that we more generously compliment virtue and effort.

A RESOLUTION

A new commandment I give unto you,
That ye love one another; as I have loved you,
that ye also love one another.

—JOHN 13:34

Let us from this day forward be a little better, love one another a little more, treat one another with greater kindness and look to God and live.

THE LAW OF TITHING

Bring ye all the tithes into the storehouse, that there
may be meat in mine house, and prove me now
herewith, saith the Lord of hosts, if I will not
open you the windows of heaven, and pour
you out a blessing, that there shall
not be room enough to receive it.

—MALACHI 3:10

Pay your tithing. Put the Lord to the test. See if He
will not open the windows of heaven and shower
down blessings upon you that you do not have
room enough to contain them. He will bless you. I
don't mean to infer that He will make you rich and
wealthy. I do mean to say without any hesitation
whatsoever, that He will bless you and bring joy
into your lives and blessings that are as real as anything on this earth.

REACHING THOSE IN NEED

I would that ye should impart of your substance to the poor, every man according to that which he hath, such as feeding the hungry, clothing the naked, visiting the sick and administering to their relief, both spiritually and temporally, according to their wants.

—MOSIAH 4:26

Reach out in love to those who need our strength. There are many among us who lie alone in pain. Medicine helps, but kind words can bring to pass miracles. Many there are who walk in frightening circumstances, fearful and unable to cope. There are good bishops and Relief Society officers who are available to help, but these cannot do it all. Each of us can and must be anxiously engaged.

THE PRIVILEGE OF A MISSION

Therefore, if ye have desires to serve God ye are
called to the work; For behold the field is white
already to harvest; and lo, he that thrusteth
in his sickle with his might, the same layeth
up in store that he perisheth not, but
bringeth salvation to his soul.

—DOCTRINE AND COVENANTS 4:3–4

I urge you to save and prepare and think of and dream of and pray for the experience of a mission in The Church of Jesus Christ of Latter-day Saints. Going on a mission is not only a duty, it is an opportunity. It is a privilege.

THE ANTITHESIS OF LOVE

Behold, I say unto you,
wickedness never was happiness.

—ALMA 41:10

Selfishness so often is the basis of money problems, which are a very serious and real factor affecting the stability of family life. Selfishness is at the root of adultery, the breaking of solemn and sacred covenants to satisfy lust. Selfishness is the antithesis of love. It is a cankering expression of greed. It destroys self-discipline. It obliterates loyalty. It tears up sacred covenants. It afflicts both men and women. Selfishness is the great destroyer of happy family life.

A SACRED COVENANT

Now I say unto you, if this be the desire of your
hearts, what have you against being baptized in
the name of the Lord, as a witness before him
that ye have entered into a covenant with
him, that ye will serve him and keep his
commandments, that he may pour out
his Spirit more abundantly upon you?

—MOSIAH 18:10

Every member of this church who has entered the waters of baptism has become a party to a sacred covenant. Each time we partake of the sacrament of the Lord's supper, we renew that covenant. We take upon ourselves anew the name of the Lord Jesus Christ and promise to keep His commandments.

KNEEL IN FAMILY PRAYER

We will give ourselves continually to prayer.

—ACTS 6:4

I feel satisfied that there is no adequate substitute for the morning and evening practice of kneeling together—father, mother, and children. This, more than heavy carpets, more than lovely draperies, more than cleverly balanced color schemes, is the thing that will make for better and more beautiful homes.

TO PARTAKE OF THE SACRAMENT

It is expedient that the church meet together often
to partake of bread and wine in the
remembrance of the Lord Jesus.

—DOCTRINE AND COVENANTS 20:75

If we will go to sacrament meeting every week and reflect as we partake of the sacrament on the meaning of the prayers, if we will listen to the language of those prayers, which were given by revelation, and live by them, we will be a better people, each of us will be. That is the importance of sacrament meeting.

WHILE THEY ARE YOUNG

And that from a child thou hast known the holy
scriptures, which are able to make thee wise unto
salvation through faith which is in Christ Jesus.

—2 TIMOTHY 3:15

Read to your children from the scriptures. They
will not understand all that you read, but they will
have a feeling in their hearts of something good
and true and precious.

AVOID DEBT

Pay the debt thou hast contracted....
Release thyself from bondage.

—DOCTRINE AND COVENANTS 19:35

We have been seduced into believing that borrowed money has no penalty, that financial bondage is an acceptable way to live. I suggest that it is not. We would do well to be modest and prudent in our expenditures, to discipline our purchasing and avoid debt to the extent possible, to pay off debt quickly, and to free ourselves from the bondage of others.

ACCOUNTABILITY

For we must all appear before the judgment seat of
Christ; that every one may receive the things done
in his body, according to that he hath done,
whether it be good or bad.

—2 CORINTHIANS 5:10

People who carry in their hearts a strong conviction concerning the living reality of the Almighty and their accountability to Him for what they do with their lives are far less likely to become enmeshed in problems that inevitably weaken society.

LIVE IN KINDNESS

Let all bitterness, and wrath, and anger, and
clamour, and evil speaking, be put away from
you, with all malice: And be ye kind one to
another, tenderhearted, forgiving one another,
even as God for Christ's sake hath forgiven you.

—EPHESIANS 4:31–32

Is it too simple a thing to wish that all of you might live lives filled with kindness? We live in a harsh and mean world. It is spoken of as "the jungle." It is often so ruthless, so heartless, so mean, so vicious. What a marvelous thing is a little human kindness.

ENLIGHTENED PROGRESS

Let us cheerfully do all things that lie in our power;
and then may we stand still, with the utmost
assurance, to see the salvation of God,
and for his arm to be revealed.

—DOCTRINE AND COVENANTS 123:17

Industry, enthusiasm, and hard work lead to enlightened progress.

Personal Refinement

*If there is anything virtuous, lovely, or of good
report or praiseworthy, we seek after these things.*

—ARTICLES OF FAITH 1:13

Sloppy language and sloppy ways go together.
Those who are truly educated have learned more
than the sciences, the humanities, law, engineering,
and the arts. They carry with them a certain polish
that marks them as loving the better qualities of
life, a culture that adds luster to the mundane
world of which they are a part, a patina that puts a
quiet glow on what otherwise might be base metal.

A SPIRIT OF GLADNESS

For I have given you an example, that ye should do
as I have done to you. . . . If ye know these
things, happy are ye if ye do them.

—JOHN 13:15, 17

Be happy in that which you do. Cultivate a spirit of gladness in your homes. Subdue and overcome all elements of anger, impatience, and unbecoming talk one to another.

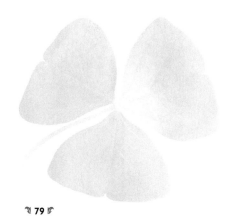

WALK IN PEACE

He who doeth the works of righteousness shall
receive his reward, even peace in this world,
and eternal life in the world to come.

—DOCTRINE AND COVENANTS 59:23

Walk in the sunlight of that peace which comes from obedience to the commandments of the Lord.

A QUIET VOICE

A soft answer turneth away wrath:
but grievous words stir up anger.

—PROVERBS 15:1

We seldom get into trouble when we speak softly. It is only when we raise our voices that the sparks fly and tiny molehills of difference become great mountains of contention. The voice of heaven is a still, small voice; likewise, the voice of domestic peace is a quiet voice.

As Sisters in Zion

*They did walk uprightly before God, imparting to
one another both temporally and spiritually
according to their needs and their wants.*

—MOSIAH 18:29

Lucy Mack Smith, mother of the Prophet, in
speaking to the sisters in Nauvoo, said, "We must
cherish one another, watch over one another, and
gain instruction that we may all sit down in heaven
together" (Minutes, 24 March 1842). The history of
Relief Society has shown that women of the
Church have not had to wait to sit together in
heaven to taste the sweet fruit of the kind of activities she described. They have experienced much
of heaven on earth as in life they have cherished
one another, comforted one another, and
instructed one another.

TRUE REPENTANCE

He who has repented of his sins, the same is
forgiven, and I, the Lord, remember
them no more.

—DOCTRINE AND COVENANTS 58:42

Where there is true repentance, there will be forgiveness. The process begins with prayer.

ETERNAL FAMILIES

Neither is the man without the woman, neither the woman without the man, in the Lord.

—1 CORINTHIANS 11:11

Our Father in Heaven, who loves His children, desires for them that which will bring them happiness now and in the eternities to come, and there is no greater happiness than is found in the most meaningful of all human relationships—the companionships of husband and wife and parents and children.

HEAVEN'S SMILE

Humble yourselves in the sight of the Lord,
and he shall lift you up.

—JAMES 4:10

Be humble and be prayerful, and the smiles of heaven will fall upon you.

A Sabbath-Keeping People

And that thou mayest more fully keep thyself
unspotted from the world, thou shalt go to the
house of prayer and offer up thy sacraments
upon my holy day; For verily this is a day
appointed unto you to rest from your labors,
and to pay thy devotions unto the Most High.

—DOCTRINE AND COVENANTS 59:9–10

The Lord wrote concerning the sanctity of the Sabbath when His finger touched the tablets of stone on Sinai: Keep the Sabbath day holy. Let us be a Sabbath-keeping people. Now I do not want to be prudish. I do not want you to lock up your children in the house and read the Bible all afternoon to them. Be wise. Be careful. But make that day a day when you can sit down with your families and talk about sacred and good things.

THE MANTLE OF THE PRIESTHOOD

*For whoso is faithful unto the obtaining these two
priesthoods of which I have spoken, and the
magnifying their calling, are sanctified by the
Spirit unto the renewing of their bodies. They
become the sons of Moses and of Aaron and
the seed of Abraham, and the church and
kingdom, and the elect of God.*

—DOCTRINE AND COVENANTS 84:33–34

It is no simple or unimportant thing to wear the
mantle of the holy priesthood in whatever office or
at whatever level and in whatever responsibility we
might be called to serve.

A NOBLE SOCIETY

He hath brought to pass the redemption of the
world, whereby he that is found guiltless before him
at the judgment day hath it given unto him to dwell
in the presence of God in his kingdom, . . . in a state
of happiness which hath no end. Therefore . . . lay
hold upon the gospel of Christ.

—MORMON 7:7–8

What a marvelous thing it is to belong to a society whose purposes are noble, whose accomplishments are tremendous, whose work is uplifting, even heroic. Be loyal to the Church under all circumstances. This is your church. You have embraced its gospel. You have taken upon yourselves a covenant in the waters of baptism. Be proud of your membership in this great cause and kingdom which He has restored to earth in this, the last dispensation of the fulness of times. Why? To bring you happiness.

SELF-DISCIPLINE

*Till I die I will not remove mine
integrity from me.*

—JOB 27:5

Permissiveness never produced greatness. Integrity, loyalty, and strength are virtues whose sinews are developed through the struggles that go on within a man as he practices self-discipline under the demands of divinely spoken truth.

LOSE YOURSELF IN SERVICE

For whoso findeth me findeth life.

—PROVERBS 8:35

Generally speaking, the most miserable people I know are those who are obsessed with themselves; the happiest people I know are those who lose themselves in the service of others. By and large, I have come to see that if we complain about life, it is because we are thinking only of ourselves.

OUR MESSAGE AND MISSION

We claim the privilege of worshiping Almighty God according to the dictates of our own conscience, and allow all men the same privilege, let them worship how, where, or what they may.

—ARTICLES OF FAITH 1:11

We recognize the good that every other church in the world does. We have no quarrel with other churches. We do not argue, we do not debate, or anything of the kind. We simply say to people not of our faith, "You bring with you all the truth that you have, and let us see if we can add to it." That is the mission and message of this church.

AN ETERNAL PERSPECTIVE

*And we know that all men must repent and believe
on the name of Jesus Christ, and worship the
Father in his name, and endure in faith on
his name to the end, or they cannot be
saved in the kingdom of God.*

—DOCTRINE AND COVENANTS 20:29

Walk in virtue and truth, with faith and faithfulness. You are part of an eternal plan, a plan designed by God our Eternal Father. Each day is a part of that eternity.

Be Believing

*And Christ hath said: If ye will have faith in me ye
shall have power to do whatsoever thing
is expedient in me.*

—MORONI 7:33

Be not faithless, but believing, in your capacity as
a son or daughter of God to learn so that you may
go forth to serve and make a contribution to the
society of which you will become a part. Look up
and go forward.

A PERSONAL TESTIMONY

Behold, I have all things as a testimony
that these things are true.

—ALMA 30:41

Personal testimony, coupled with performance,
cannot be refuted.

APRIL

There is a resurrection,
therefore the grave hath
no victory, and the sting
of death is swallowed
up in Christ.

—MOSIAH 16:8

THE BEST ANTIDOTE

The power is in them, wherein they are agents unto
themselves. And inasmuch as men do good they
shall in nowise lose their reward.

—DOCTRINE AND COVENANTS 58:28

The best antidote I know for worry is work.

The best medicine for despair is service.

The best cure for weariness is the challenge of
helping someone who is even more tired.

EXERCISE SELF-CONTROL

Cease from anger, and forsake wrath.

—PSALM 37:8

Discipline yourself. Master your temper. Most of the things that make you angry are of very small consequence. And what a terrible price you pay for anger. Ask the Lord to forgive you. Ask your family members to forgive you. Apologize and resolve to exercise more self-control.

ACHIEVING GREATNESS

But he that believeth these things which I have spoken, him will I visit with the manifestations of my Spirit, and he shall know and bear record. For because of my Spirit he shall know that these things are true; for it persuadeth men to do good.

—ETHER 4:11

Great buildings were never constructed on uncertain foundations. Great causes were never brought to success by vacillating leaders. The gospel was never expounded to the convincing of others without certainty. Without certitude on the part of believers, a religious cause becomes soft, without muscle, without the driving force that would broaden its influence and capture the hearts and affections of men and women.

LOOK FOR VIRTUE

Finally, be ye all of one mind, having compassion
one of another, love as brethren, be pitiful, be
courteous: Not rendering evil for evil, or railing
for railing: but contrariwise blessing; knowing that
ye are thereunto called, that ye should inherit a
blessing. For he that will love life, and see good
days, let him refrain his tongue from evil,
and his lips that they speak no guile.

—1 PETER 3:8–10

If we will look for the virtues in one another and not the vices, there will be much more of happiness in the homes of our people. There will be far less of divorce, much less of infidelity, much less of anger and rancor and quarreling. There will be more of forgiveness, more of love, more of peace, more of happiness. This is as the Lord would have it.

TRUST IN THE LORD

Trust in the Lord with all thine heart; and lean not unto thine own understanding. In all thy ways acknowledge him, and he shall direct thy paths.

—PROVERBS 3:5–6

If ye are prepared ye shall not fear" (D&C 38:30). This brief statement is a promise wonderful and sure. It carries a message for all of us—for the youth who wonders about education, for the head of the household who has responsibility for a family, for the business or professional man, for the teacher or the speaker, for the church officer. All of us occasionally face responsibilities that bring with them a sense of fear. Where there is adequate preparation, there need be no fear. Such is the promise of the Lord.

GENERAL CONFERENCE

I will praise the Lord with my whole heart, in the
assembly of the upright, and in the congregation.

—PSALM 111:1

General conferences are held to strengthen our testimonies of this work, to fortify us against temptation and sin, to lift our sights, to receive instruction concerning the programs of the Church and the pattern of our lives.

A GREAT WORK

For of him unto whom much is given much is required.

—DOCTRINE AND COVENANTS 82:3

Our membership in The Church of Jesus Christ of Latter-day Saints is a precious thing. It isn't a simple or ordinary thing; this is the church and kingdom of God. This is the kingdom of God on earth. This is His work in which we are engaged and there is no more important work in all the world than this work. It concerns the eternal salvation of the sons and daughters of God, those living, those who have lived upon the earth, and those who will yet live. No people have ever been charged with a greater, more inclusive mandate than we have, you and I. Our work, given to us by the Lord, encompasses all of mankind.

CEASE TO BE IDLE

Thou shalt not be idle; for he that is idle shall
not eat the bread nor wear the
garments of the laborer.

—DOCTRINE AND COVENANTS 42:42

Without hard work, nothing grows but weeds.

AN ETERNAL INVESTMENT

And, if you keep my commandments and endure to
the end you shall have eternal life, which gift is
the greatest of all the gifts of God.

—DOCTRINE AND COVENANTS 14:7

It is not a sacrifice to live the gospel of Jesus Christ. It is never a sacrifice when you get back more than you give. It is an investment. And the living of the gospel of Jesus Christ becomes a greater investment than any of which we know because its dividends are eternal and everlasting.

PURE IN HEART

But now ye also put off all these; anger, wrath,
malice, blasphemy, filthy communication
out of your mouth.

—COLOSSIANS 3:8

There is no room in the heart of a Latter-day Saint for bitterness, for unkindness, for animosity to any other of the sons and daughters of God.

DEDICATED SERVICE

Not with eyeservice, as menpleasers; but as the
servants of Christ, doing the will of God from
the heart; With good will doing service,
as to the Lord, and not to men.

—EPHESIANS 6:6–7

Truly great men and women resolve to dedicate
a part of their lives and time to those in distress.
Helping hands can lift someone out of the mire of
difficulty. Steady voices can provide encouragement for some who might otherwise simply give
up. Skills can change, in a remarkable and wonderful way, the lives of those in need. It is not enough
for any of us to get a job and feverishly work
to produce income that leads only to personal
comfort. We may gain some recompense in all of
this, but we will not gain the ultimate satisfaction.
When we serve others, we best serve our God.

LIVE KINDLY

Beloved, let us love one another: for love is of God;
and every one that loveth is born of God,
and knoweth God.

—1 JOHN 4:7

Let us, each of us, watch ourselves. Whenever we
have within us a little temper, go outside, breathe
some fresh air, and come in with a smile and throw
your arms around your companion, and tell her
you love her. Look to your children and let them
know that you love them. Live with them kindly
and graciously, as Latter-day Saints should do.

HAPPY IN THE WORK

Wherefore I perceive that there is nothing better,
than that a man should rejoice in his own works;
for that is his portion: for who shall bring him
to see what shall be after him?

—ECCLESIASTES 3:22

Love the work. Don't do it grudgingly. Smile about it. Be happy in doing your duty. Shape up and say your prayers. Everything will be all right.

AN ENSIGN TO THE NATIONS

Verily I say unto you all: Arise and shine forth,
that thy light may be a standard for the nations.

—DOCTRINE AND COVENANTS 115:5

Beginning with you and me, there can be an
entire people who, by the virtue of our lives in our
homes, in our vocations, even in our amusements,
can become as a city upon a hill to which men may
look and learn, and an ensign to the nations from
which the people of the earth may gather strength.

THE ASSURANCE OF IMMORTALITY

*I am the resurrection, and the life: he that believeth
in me, though he were dead, yet shall he live:
And whosoever liveth and believeth
in me shall never die.*

—JOHN 11:25–26

There is nothing more universal than death, and
nothing brighter with hope and faith than the
assurance of immortality. The abject sorrow that
comes with death, the bereavement that follows the
passing of a loved one are mitigated only by the
certainty of the resurrection of the Son of God that
first Easter morning, bringing the assurance that
all will rise from the grave.

HE REMEMBERS THEM NO MORE

For I will be merciful to their unrighteousness,
and their sins and their iniquities will
I remember no more.

—HEBREWS 8:12

Eternal vigilance is the price of eternal development. Occasionally we may stumble. I thank the Lord for the great principle of repentance and forgiveness. When we drop the ball, when we make a mistake, there is held out to us the word of the Lord that He will forgive our sins and remember them no more against us.

ONE GREAT FAMILY

Thou shalt not avenge, nor bear any grudge against
the children of thy people, but thou shalt love
thy neighbour as thyself: I am the Lord.

—LEVITICUS 19:18

We speak of the fellowship of the Saints. This is and must be a very real thing. We must never permit this spirit of brotherhood and sisterhood to weaken. We must constantly cultivate it. Simply put, we must be friends. We must love and honor and respect and assist one another. Wherever Latter-day Saints go, they are made welcome, because Latter-day Saints are mutual believers in the divinity of the Lord Jesus Christ and are engaged together in His great cause. We are one great family, eleven million strong.

EXPECTATIONS

If thou lovest me thou shalt serve me.

—DOCTRINE AND COVENANTS 42:29

God expects us to develop in our hearts and lives a profound love for the Lord Jesus Christ, the Savior and the Redeemer of the world. That will find its best expression in the service we give to others.

"DOUBT NOT, FEAR NOT"

Look unto me in every thought;
doubt not, fear not.

—DOCTRINE AND COVENANTS 6:36

If we will be prayerful, seeking wisdom from God, who is the source of all true wisdom, we shall be blessed as God has promised. Our Father has made explicit covenants with His people. He is in a position to keep those covenants. We have nothing to fear if we stay on the Lord's side.

READ THE SCRIPTURES

And it shall be with him, and he shall read therein
all the days of his life: that he may learn to fear
the Lord his God, to keep all the words of
this law and these statutes, to do them.

—DEUTERONOMY 17:19

Let us establish in our lives the habit of reading those things which will strengthen our faith in the Lord Jesus Christ, the Savior of the world.

TEACH CHILDREN TO PRAY

Counsel with the Lord in all thy doings, and he will direct thee for good; yea, when thou liest down at night lie down unto the Lord, . . . and when thou risest in the morning let thy heart be full of thanks unto God; and if ye do these things, ye shall be lifted up at the last day.

—ALMA 37:37

Teach children how to pray concerning their own needs and righteous desires. Let prayer, night and morning, as a family and as individuals, become a practice in which children grow while yet young. There will distill into their hearts a natural inclination in times of distress and extremity to turn to God as their Father and friend.

ALL ARE CHILDREN OF GOD

The Spirit itself beareth witness with our spirit,
that we are the children of God.

—ROMANS 8:16

There is no need in any land for conflict between diverse groups of any kind. Let there be taught in the homes of people that we are all children of God, our Eternal Father, and that as surely as there is fatherhood, there can and must be brotherhood.

A BETTER LIFE

*Consider on the blessed and happy state of those
that keep the commandments of God. For behold,
they are blessed in all things, both temporal and
spiritual; and if they hold out faithful to the
end they are received into heaven, that
thereby they may dwell with God in
a state of never-ending happiness.*

—MOSIAH 2:41

What a wonderful thing is death, really, when all is said and done. It is the great reliever. It is a majestic, quiet passing on from this life to another life, a better life. We go to a place where we will not suffer as we have suffered here, but where we will continue to grow, accumulating knowledge and developing and being useful under the plan of the Almighty made possible through the atonement of the Son of God.

No Ordinary Cause

That the kingdoms of this world may be
constrained to acknowledge that the kingdom
of Zion is in very deed the kingdom of our
God and his Christ; therefore, let us
become subject unto her laws.

—DOCTRINE AND COVENANTS 105:32

This cause in which we are engaged is not an ordinary cause. It is the cause of Christ. It is the kingdom of God our Eternal Father. It is the building of Zion on the earth, the fulfillment of prophecy given of old and of a vision revealed in this dispensation.

"An Heritage of the Lord"

Lo, children are an heritage of the Lord: and the fruit of the womb is his reward. As arrows are in the hand of a mighty man; so are children of the youth. Happy is the man that hath his quiver full of them.

—PSALM 127:3–5

How much more beautiful would be the world and the societies in which we live if every father and mother looked upon their children as the most precious of their assets, if they led them by the power of their example in kindness and love, and if in times of stress blessed them by the authority of the holy priesthood, and if they regarded their children as the jewels of their lives, as gifts from the God of heaven who is their Eternal Father, and brought them up with true affection in the wisdom and admonition of the Lord.

THERE IS WORK TO DO

The Lord hath brought forth our righteousness:
come, and let us declare in Zion the work
of the Lord our God.

—JEREMIAH 51:10

We have work to do, you and I, so very much of it. Let us roll up our sleeves and get at it, with a new commitment, putting our trust in the Lord.

RISE TO YOUR POTENTIAL

A gracious woman retaineth honour.

—PROVERBS 11:16

I feel to invite every woman everywhere to rise to the great potential within you. I do not ask that you reach beyond your capacity. I hope you will not nag yourselves with thoughts of failure. I hope you will not try to set goals far beyond your capacity to achieve. I hope you will simply do what you can do in the best way you know. If you do so, you will witness miracles come to pass.

SACRIFICE FOR THE LORD

Behold, now it is called today until the coming of the Son of Man, and verily it is a day of sacrifice.

—DOCTRINE AND COVENANTS 64:23

Our willingness to sacrifice for this the Lord's work reminds us that this is the very essence of the Atonement, the ultimate sacrifice made by the Son of God in behalf of each of us.

A PLACE OF COVENANTS

And verily I say unto you, let this house be built
unto my name, that I may reveal mine ordinances
therein unto my people; For I deign to reveal unto
my church things which have been kept hid from
before the foundation of the world, things that
pertain to the dispensation of the fulness of times.

—DOCTRINE AND COVENANTS 124:40–41

The temple is a place of covenants. In the house of the Lord, we take upon ourselves covenants and obligations regarding lives of purity and virtue and goodness and truth and unselfishness to others. Through these covenants we have a special relationship with God our Eternal Father, eternal and everlasting if we live worthy of it.

CHILDREN OF ABRAHAM

*Know ye therefore that they which are of faith, the
same are the children of Abraham.... So then they
which be of faith are blessed with faithful Abraham.*

—GALATIANS 3:7, 9

I do not worry whether people are or are not
literal descendants of Israel. Whether they get their
blessings by inherited birthright or by adoption,
the end result is the same—they become partakers
of the everlasting covenant between Jehovah and
Abraham, which extends to all of his posterity,
whether by literal descent or by adoption.

MAY

A man may have great
power given him
from God.

— MOSIAH 8:16

Be Complimentary

I rejoice therefore that I have confidence
in you in all things.
—2 CORINTHIANS 7:16

Desist from making cutting remarks one to
another. Rather, cultivate the art of complimenting,
of strengthening, of encouraging. It is a responsibility divinely laid upon each of us to bear one
another's burdens, strengthen one another, to
encourage one another, to lift one another, to look
for the good in one another and to emphasize that
good. There is not a man or woman in this vast
assembly who cannot be depressed on the one
hand or lifted on the other by the remarks of his or
her associates

ATTEND THE TEMPLE

I will manifest myself to my people . . . in this house.
—DOCTRINE AND COVENANTS 110:7

Every time you go to the temple, you will be a better man or woman when you leave than you were when you came. I believe that with all my heart. I make you that promise. Redouble your efforts and your faithfulness in going to the temple and the Lord will bless you. You will be happier.

SPEAK NO EVIL

Let all . . . evil speaking, be put away from you.

—EPHESIANS 4:31

The Lord has commanded this people, saying: "Strengthen your brethren in all your conversation, in all your prayers, in all your exhortations, and in all your doings. And behold, and lo, I am with you to bless you and deliver you forever" (D&C 108:7–8). All of us have far too much to do to waste our time and energies in criticism, fault-finding, or the abuse of others. The Lord has commanded us to refrain from these things. And then follows the marvelous promise that He will bless us and deliver us forever.

A GOOD HOME

No power or influence can or ought to be
maintained by virtue of the priesthood, only
by persuasion, by long-suffering, by gentleness
and meekness, and by love unfeigned.

—DOCTRINE AND COVENANTS 121:41

Good homes are not easily created or maintained. They require discipline, not so much of children as of self. They require respect for others, that respect which comes best from acceptance of the revealed word of the Lord concerning the purpose of life, of the importance and sacred nature of the family, and recognition of each member of the family as a child of God.

THE PRINCIPLE OF THE FAST

But this is not all; they had given themselves to
much prayer, and fasting; therefore they had the
spirit of prophecy, and the spirit of revelation,
and when they taught, they taught with
power and authority of God.

—ALMA 17:3

Is it too much to ask of anyone, any member of this Church, that you actually fast for two meals a month? It will only bless our lives if we do so. I am satisfied that if every man and woman and child in the United States of America were to observe this great and marvelous practice, which costs no one anything, not a thing, that it would take care of all the welfare problems of this nation. The Lord's way is a simple way that takes nothing from us, adds to our humility, to our spirit of worship, to our physical well-being, and takes care of those in need and in distress.

YOUR GREATEST ASSETS

Little children are holy, being sanctified
through the atonement of Jesus Christ.

—DOCTRINE AND COVENANTS 74:7

Mothers and fathers, do the best you can, and remember that the greatest assets you have in this world are those children whom you have brought into the world and for whose nurture and care you are responsible.

THE STRONGEST GENERATION

I will go in the strength of the Lord.

—PSALM 71:16

We have never had a stronger generation of young men and women than we have today. Surrounded by the forces that would pull them down and tremendous pressures to pull them away from time-tested virtues, they are going forward with constructive lives, nurturing themselves both intellectually and spiritually. We have no fears or doubts concerning their future.

OUR GREATEST NEED

By the power of their words many were brought
before the altar of God, to call on his name and
confess their sins before him.

—ALMA 17:4

The greatest need of the world is a generation of
men and women of learning and influence who
can and will stand up and go forth and, in sincerity and without equivocation, declare that God
lives and that Jesus is the Christ and that all men
are brothers, with an obligation to serve one
another.

TEACH YOUR CHILDREN

*And these words, which I command thee this day,
shall be in thine heart: And thou shalt teach them
diligently unto thy children, and shalt talk of
them when thou sittest in thine house, and
when thou walkest by the way, and when
thou liest down, and when thou risest up.*

—DEUTERONOMY 6:6–7

Parents and children, teach and learn goodness
together, work together, read good books together,
pray together. These things can be done notwithstanding the frenetic pressures of our lives. They
can be done with children and particularly when
children are young.

THE POWER OF THE PRIESTHOOD

The rights of the priesthood are inseparably
connected with the powers of heaven, and . . .
the powers of heaven cannot be controlled
nor handled only upon the principles
of righteousness.

—DOCTRINE AND COVENANTS 121:36

The priesthood is not a passive thing. It is an active power. It is ours to enjoy, to exercise for the blessings of others, to magnify by the manner of our lives, and to advance the cause of the Almighty.

DAUGHTERS OF ZION

Rejoice greatly, O daughter of Zion.

—ZECHARIAH 9:9

Put on thy beautiful garments, O daughters of Zion. Live up to the great and magnificent inheritance which the Lord God, your Father in Heaven, has provided you. Rise above the dust of the world. Know that you are daughters of God, children with a divine birthright. Walk in the sun with your heads high. Know that you are loved and honored, that you are part of His kingdom, and that there is for you a great work to be done which cannot be left to others.

BROTHERHOOD

Love the brotherhood.

—1 PETER 2:17

I know of no better place to find fellowship and good friends than among the quorums of the Church. Where on earth should there be a better association than in a quorum, each of whose members is ordained to act in the name of the Lord, dedicated to help one another, and whose officers are set apart to this purpose under divine authority? Brethren, the quorums of the Church need your talents, your loyalty, your devotion; and each man needs the fellowship and blessings that come of quorum activity in the kingdom of God.

VICTORY OVER DEATH

And he hath brought to pass the redemption of the
world, whereby he that is found guiltless before
him at the judgment day hath it given unto him
to dwell in the presence of God in his kingdom,
to sing ceaseless praises with the choirs above,
unto the Father, and unto the Son, and unto
the Holy Ghost, which are one God, in a
state of happiness which hath no end.

—MORMON 7:7

Of all the victories in human history, none is so great, none so universal in its effect, none so everlasting in its consequences as the victory of the crucified Lord, who came forth in the resurrection that first Easter morning.

ASK FOR FORGIVENESS

Therefore, blessed are they who will repent and
hearken unto the voice of the Lord their God;
for these are they that shall be saved.

—HELAMAN 12:23

This is the time, this is the very hour, to repent of
any evil in the past, to ask for forgiveness, to stand
a little taller, and then to go forward with confidence and faith.

THE PRIESTHOOD OF GOD

Upon you my fellow servants, in the name of
Messiah I confer the Priesthood of Aaron, which
holds the keys of the ministering of angels, and of
the gospel of repentance, and of baptism by
immersion for the remission of sins.

—DOCTRINE AND COVENANTS 13:1

Have you ever realized that in the holding and exercise of this priesthood you are a fellow servant with John the Baptist, the very man who, while he was alive, baptized Jesus, the Savior of the world and the Son of God, in the waters of the River Jordan?

To me there is something wonderful in this. It speaks of the true spirit of the great and magnificent brotherhood of which we are all a part, the priesthood of God.

LIFE AFTER DEATH

*There is . . . a time to every
purpose under the heaven.*

—ECCLESIASTES 3:1

We are here for a purpose. We shall live after we die, and all of it is a part of eternity, and the key to everlasting life is the Atonement wrought by the Savior.

TRUE TO THE CAUSE

And they were exceedingly valiant for courage, and also for strength and activity; but behold, this was not all—they were men who were true at all times in whatsoever thing they were entrusted.

—ALMA 53:20

The Lord expects that we will be good people, clean and decent, and rise above the sins of the world, and stand tall and strong, and live the gospel in its fullness. He expects us to conduct ourselves in such a way as to bring honor and respect to His great cause and kingdom. He expects us to live the gospel as those who have taken upon themselves a great and solemn and wonderful covenant.

MAGNIFY THY CALLING

Keep these sayings, for they are true and faithful;
and thou shalt magnify thine office.

—DOCTRINE AND COVENANTS 66:11

If you will accept every call that comes to you within the Church, you will grow in a remarkable and marvelous and wonderful way. With responsibility comes growth, and the Lord will magnify you and make you equal to every responsibility which is given you.

NURTURE NEW CONVERTS

*Art thou a brother or brethren? I salute you in the
name of the Lord Jesus Christ, in token or
remembrance of the everlasting covenant, in
which covenant I receive you to fellowship, in a
determination that is fixed, immovable, and
unchangeable, to be your friend and brother
through the grace of God in the bonds of love,
to walk in all the commandments of God
blameless, in thanksgiving, forever and ever.*

—DOCTRINE AND COVENANTS 88:133

Those who have come into the Church made a
great sacrifice, many of them when they were baptized. They are precious. They are the same kind of
people that you are, and their generations will
become the same kind of people as your generations if they are nurtured and brought along in the
Church.

CHOICES AND CONSEQUENCES

Choose ye this day, to serve the
Lord God who made you.

—MOSES 6:33

Have you ever looked at a great farm gate that opens and closes? If you look at the hinge, it moves ever so little. Just a little movement of that hinge creates tremendous consequences out on the perimeter. That is the way it is with our lives. It is the little decisions that make the great differences in our lives.

LIVING WITH PURPOSE

But seek ye first the kingdom of God, and his
righteousness; and all these things shall
be added unto you.

—MATTHEW 6:33

There must be purpose in our lives. We are here to accomplish something, to bless society with our talents and our learning. There can be fun, yes. But there must be recognition of the fact that life is serious, that the risks are great, but that we can overcome them if we will discipline ourselves and seek the unfailing strength of the Lord.

GUARD AGAINST DIVISIVENESS

Be determined in one mind and in one heart.

—2 NEPHI 1:21

The enemy of truth would divide us and cultivate within us attitudes of criticism, which if permitted to prevail will only deter us in the pursuit of our divinely given goal. We cannot afford to permit it to happen. We must close ranks and march shoulder to shoulder. No power on earth can stop this work if we so conduct ourselves.

Be Humble

Let us draw near with a true heart in full assurance
of faith, having our hearts sprinkled from an evil
conscience, and our bodies washed with pure water.

—HEBREWS 10:22

Be thou humble; and the Lord thy God shall lead thee by the hand, and give thee answer to thy prayers" (D&C 112:10). What a tremendous promise is given in this statement. If we are without conceit and pride and arrogance, if we are humble and obedient, then the Lord will lead us by the hand and answer our prayers. What greater thing could we ask for? There is nothing to compare with this.

ETERNAL DIVIDENDS

He that findeth his life shall lose it:
and he that loseth his life for my sake shall find it.

—MATTHEW 10:39

The Church may call upon you to make sacrifices. It may call upon you to give of the very best that you have to offer. There will be no cost in this, because you will discover that it will become an investment that will pay you dividends for as long as you live.

"LOOK TO GOD AND LIVE"

The words of Christ, if we follow their course, [will]
carry us beyond this vale of sorrow into
a far better land of promise.

—ALMA 37:45

It is so easy to stumble. It is sometimes so hard to keep our voices low when small things provoke us. May we resolve in our hearts to live the gospel, to be faithful and true, to have the strength to look above small things that could lead to argument and trouble, to be forgiving of one another, to "look to God and live" (Alma 37:47).

THE SUNLIGHT OF LOVE

And if ye do this with a pure heart, in all faithfulness, ye shall be blessed; you shall be blessed in your flocks, and in your herds, and in your fields, and in your houses, and in your families.

—DOCTRINE AND COVENANTS 136:11

No family can have peace, no home can be free from storms of adversity, unless that family and that home are built on foundations of morality, fidelity, and mutual respect. There cannot be peace where there is not trust; there cannot be freedom where there is not loyalty. The warm sunlight of love will not rise out of a swamp or immorality.

THE SPIRIT OF FREEDOM

*The Spirit of God . . .
is also the spirit of freedom.*

—ALMA 61:15

The gospel is not a philosophy of repression, as so many regard it. It is a plan of freedom that gives discipline to appetite and direction to behavior.

"Cease to Find Fault"

Cease to find fault one with another.

—DOCTRINE AND COVENANTS 88:124

None of us is perfect; all of us occasionally make mistakes. There was only one perfect individual who ever walked the earth. Men and women who carry heavy responsibility do not need criticism, they need encouragement. One can disagree with policy without being disagreeable concerning the policy maker.

REDEEMING THE DEAD

The building of the temples and the performance of ordinances therein for the redemption of the dead, were also in the spirit world.

—DOCTRINE AND COVENANTS 138:54

The mystery of death has been the eminent concern of thoughtful men and women of all ages. The work in the temple, based on the atonement of the Savior of mankind, is the one sure answer to that mystery. It brings light and understanding. It brings hope and assurance. It brings conviction and faith.

TAKE TIME TO SERVE

Inasmuch as ye have done it unto one of the least of these my brethren, ye have done it unto me.

—MATTHEW 25:40

One of the greatest challenges we face in our hurried, self-centered lives is to follow the counsel of the Master "to do it unto one of the least of these my brethren." Take the time today to reach out, to help someone less fortunate, to strengthen and lift a brother or sister in need.

THE BURDEN OF DEBT

The borrower is servant to the lender.

—PROVERBS 22:7

Debt can be a terrible thing. It is so easy to incur and so difficult to repay. I hasten to add that borrowing under some circumstances is necessary. Perhaps you need to borrow to complete your education. If you do, see that you pay it back. And do so promptly even at the sacrifice of some comforts that you might otherwise enjoy. You likely will have to borrow in securing a home. But be wise and do not go beyond your ability to pay. Borrowed money is had only at a price, and that price can be burdensome.

JUNE

*The light of the body is
the eye; if, therefore, thine
eye be single, thy whole
body shall be full of light.*

—3 NEPHI 13:22

YOUR DIVINE NATURE

Be ye therefore perfect, even as your Father
which is in heaven is perfect.

—MATTHEW 5:48

Believe in yourself. Believe in your capacity to do great and good and worthwhile things. Believe in the nature within you, the divine nature, that you are in very deed a son or daughter of the living God. There is something of divinity within you, something that stands high and tall and noble. Get above the dirt and the filth of the earth and walk on a higher plane with your heads up, believing in yourselves and in your capacity to act for good in the world and make a difference.

AVOID CRITICISM

And now abideth faith, hope, charity, these three;
but the greatest of these is charity.
—1 CORINTHIANS 13:13

Criticism is the forerunner of divorce, the culti-
vator of rebellion, a catalyst that leads to failure. I
am asking that we turn from the negative that so
permeates our society and look for the remarkable
good among those with whom we associate, that
we speak of one another's virtues more than we
speak of one another's faults, that optimism replace
pessimism, that our faith exceed our fears. When I
was a young man and was prone to speak critically,
my father would say: "Cynics do not contribute,
skeptics do not create, doubters do not achieve."

"Love Thy Neighbour"

Thou shalt love the Lord thy God with all thy heart,
and with all thy soul, and with all thy mind.
This is the first and great commandment.
And the second is like unto it, Thou
shalt love thy neighbour as thyself.

—MATTHEW 22:37–39

The Lord expects we will be good neighbors, kind to others, to those not of our faith; that we will treat them with generosity and love and respect; that when they have troubles, we will reach out to assist them and help and bless them. The God of Heaven expects us to be friends to all within our reach.

THE YOUTH OF THE CHURCH

Let no man despise thy youth; but be thou an
example of the believers, in word, in conversation,
in charity, in spirit, in faith, in purity.

—1 TIMOTHY 4:12

I have tremendous confidence in the young people of this Church. I love you. I believe in you. I have every confidence that you are going to do the right thing; that you are going to make a go of life; that you are going to make a contribution to society; that you are going to live the kind of lives that are productive and produce wonderful results. Notwithstanding all of the temptations that you face, I believe that you are the greatest generation we have ever had in this Church.

"Lifted Up at the Last Day"

Whosoever shall put their trust in God shall be
supported in their trials, and their troubles,
and their afflictions, and shall be lifted
up at the last day.

—ALMA 36:3

We may know much of loneliness. We may know discouragement and frustration. We may know adversity and trouble and pain. I would hope not. But you know, and I know, that suffering comes to many. Sometimes it is mental. Sometimes it is physical. Sometimes it may even be spiritual. Ours is the duty to walk by faith, rising above the evils and trials of the world. We are sons and daughters of God. Ours is a divine birthright. Ours is a divine destiny.

THE ATONEMENT

For I know that my redeemer liveth, and that he
shall stand at the latter day upon the earth: And
though after my skin worms destroy this body,
yet in my flesh shall I see God.

—JOB 19:25–26

None of us fully understands the Atonement. I think it is beyond the comprehension of any man. But we know something of it, and we know that as a result of it we will be resurrected from the grave, and that those who walk in obedience to His commandments will be given the opportunity of going on to eternal exaltation.

ALIVE IN CHRIST

*For as in Adam all die, even so in Christ
shall all be made alive.*

—1 CORINTHIANS 15:22

As mortals we all must die. Death is as much a part of eternal life as is birth. Looked at through mortal eyes, without comprehension of the eternal plan of God, death is a bleak, final, and unrelenting experience. But our Eternal Father, whose children we are, made possible a far better thing through the sacrifice of His Only Begotten Son, the Lord Jesus Christ. Can anyone believe that the Great Creator would provide for life and growth and achievement only to snuff it all into oblivion in the process of death? Reason says no. Justice demands a better answer. The God of heaven has given one. The Lord Jesus Christ provided it.

Do Away with Anger

Behold, this is not my doctrine, to stir up the hearts
of men with anger, one against another; but this is
my doctrine, that such things should be done away.

—3 NEPHI 11:30

The flower of love fades in an atmosphere of criticism and carping, of mean words and uncontrolled anger. Love flies out the window when contention enters.

TRUE REWARDS

The soul of the sluggard desireth, and hath nothing:
but the soul of the diligent shall be made fat.

—PROVERBS 13:4

There is nothing in all the world so satisfying as a task well done. There is no reward so pleasing as that which comes from the mastery of a difficult problem or challenge.

AN EXEMPLARY FATHER

And, ye fathers, provoke not your children to wrath: but bring them up in the nurture and admonition of the Lord.

—EPHESIANS 6:4

The father is the provider, the defender, the counselor, the friend who will listen and give support when needed. Who better than an exemplary father to effectively teach children the value of education, the dead-end nature of street gangs, and the miracle of self-esteem that can change their lives for good?

COUNSEL TO MISSIONARIES

Let your light so shine before men, that they may see your good works, and glorify your Father which is in heaven.

—MATTHEW 5:16

To missionaries: Go forward. Do your work. It's so very, very important. You have on your narrow shoulders the responsibility of teaching the gospel to a world that doesn't want it. At least they think they don't want it because they haven't tasted of it. And for many, many of those people you are the only source of knowledge they will ever have of this Church. It is so very important, therefore, that you make a good appearance. Someday someone might well say, "Well, yes, I met two of your missionaries years ago and I've been thinking about it ever since then. Come in and tell me what you have to offer." Go forward with faith and without fear.

BE WORTHY

The Lord will give grace and glory: no good thing
will he withhold from them that walk uprightly.

—PSALM 84:11

Shape up. I say that to myself constantly. Shape up. Stand a little taller. Be a little better, a little stronger, a little more thoughtful, a little humbler, a little more prayerful, that you may be worthy of the guidance of the Lord and of His wonderful blessings.

Behold Your Little Ones

And he spake unto the multitude, and said unto them: Behold your little ones. And as they looked to behold they cast their eyes towards heaven, and they saw the heavens open, and they saw angels descending out of heaven as it were in the midst of fire; and they came down and encircled those little ones about, . . . and the angels did minister unto them.

—3 NEPHI 17:23–24

Behold your little ones. Pray with them. Pray for them and bless them. The world into which they are moving is a complex and difficult world. They will run into heavy seas of adversity. They will need all the strength and all the faith you can give them. They must lift their world, and the only levers they will have are the examples in their own lives and the powers of persuasion that will come of your testimonies and your knowledge of the things of God.

BLESS THIS NATION

Have mercy, O Lord, upon all the nations of the earth; have mercy upon the rulers of our land; may those principles, which were so honorably and nobly defended, namely, the Constitution of our land, by our fathers, be established forever.

—DOCTRINE AND COVENANTS 109:54

May God bless this nation of which you and I are a part. Bless her leaders that they may rise above pettiness and live after the tradition of the Founding Fathers. Bless our industry that it may benefit all mankind. Bless our science that out of it may come health and happiness for the peoples of the earth. Bless the people of this nation, you, every one of you, and me, and all who walk beneath its glorious flag with gratitude and appreciation, with respect and reverence, as well as with love.

A Time and a Season

To every thing there is a season.

—ECCLESIASTES 3:1

There are seasons in our lives, seasons when we can prepare and work, when the sun shines and the air is warm. And there are other seasons when the storms of life would beat upon us and destroy us if they could. Summer is the time of preparation against the harshness of winter.

BE CLEAN

*Whosoever committeth sin
is the servant of sin.*

—JOHN 8:34

Youth is the seedtime for the future flowering of family life. To hope for peace and love and gladness out of promiscuity is to hope for that which will never come. To wish for freedom out of immorality is to wish for something that cannot be.

SERVE OTHERS

*And behold, I tell you these things that ye may
learn wisdom; that ye may learn that when ye are
in the service of your fellow beings ye are only
in the service of your God.*

—MOSIAH 2:17

No man can be a true Latter-day Saint who is
unneighborly, who does not reach out to assist and
help others. It is inherent in the very nature of the
gospel that we do so. My brothers and sisters, we
cannot live unto ourselves. The more we forget
ourselves and lose ourselves in the service of
others, the closer we draw to the Lord and His
great work and kingdom.

Be Honest

Lying lips are abomination to the Lord:
but they that deal truly are his delight.

—PROVERBS 12:22

Be honest. It is such a simple thing, and yet so very difficult for so many people. Great is the man, regardless of his other accomplishments, who is known as one of integrity, on whose word all can depend. Said Shakespeare, "To thine own self be true; and it must follow as the night and the day, thou canst not then be false to any man" (*Hamlet,* 1.iii,78–81). Churchill once said that the first victim of war is truth. It seems, in so very many cases, that it is also the first victim of business and other activities.

INTEGRITY

The fruit of the righteous is a tree of life;
and he that winneth souls is wise.

—PROVERBS 11:30

In our day, those found in dishonesty aren't put to death, but something within them dies. Conscience chokes, character withers, self-respect vanishes, and integrity dies. Without honesty, our lives disintegrate into ugliness, chaos, and a lack of any kind of security and confidence.

THE ENVIRONMENT OF THE HOME

And again, you shall . . . do the work of printing,
and of selecting and writing books for schools in
this church, that little children also may receive
instruction before me as is pleasing unto me.

—DOCTRINE AND COVENANTS 55:4

Parents, work at the matter of creating an exciting atmosphere in your homes. Let your children be exposed to great minds, great ideas, everlasting truth, and those things which will build and motivate for good.

TEMPLE BUILDING

*And inasmuch as my people build a house unto me
in the name of the Lord, and do not suffer any
unclean thing to come into it, that it be not
defiled, my glory shall rest upon it; Yea,
and my presence shall be there.*

—DOCTRINE AND COVENANTS 97:15–16

The blessings of the temple represent that fulness of the priesthood of which the Lord spoke when He revealed His will unto the Prophet Joseph Smith. The construction of each temple represents a maturing of the Church. We will continue to build these sacred houses of the Lord as rapidly as energy and resources will allow. We are grateful for the faithful Latter-day Saints who pay their tithing and make possible these temples.

DON'T GIVE UP ON THEM

Use boldness, but not overbearance; and
also see that ye bridle all your passions,
that ye may be filled with love.

—ALMA 38:12

To any who have sons and daughters who stray, may I suggest that you never quit trying. They are never lost until you have given up. Remember that it is love, more than any other thing, that will bring them back. Punishment is not likely to do it. Reprimands without love will not accomplish it. Patience, expressions of appreciation, and that strange and remarkable power which comes with prayer will eventually win through.

Choosing the Right

Wherefore, men are free according to the flesh; and all things are given them which are expedient unto man. And they are free to choose liberty and eternal life, through the great Mediator of all men, or to choose captivity and death, according to the captivity and power of the devil; for he seeketh that all men might be miserable like unto himself.

—2 NEPHI 2:27

The ancient premortal struggle continues, the unrelenting battle that comes of free agency. Some, unfortunately, choose the wrong. But many, so many, choose the right, including so very many of our choice young men and young women. They deserve and need our gratitude. They need our encouragement. They need the kind of examples that we can become before them.

THE PURSUIT OF TESTIMONY

If any man will do his will, he shall know of the
doctrine, whether it be of God, or whether
I speak of myself.

—JOHN 7:17

The gaining of a strong and secure testimony is the privilege and opportunity of every individual member of the Church. Service in behalf of others, study, and prayer lead to faith in this work and then to knowledge of its truth. This has always been a personal pursuit, as it must always be in the future.

LOVE THE WORD OF GOD

*He that will not harden his heart, to him is given
the greater portion of the word, until it is given
unto him to know the mysteries of God
until he know them in full.*

—ALMA 12:10

I hope the reading of scriptures will become something far more enjoyable than a duty; that, rather, it will become a love affair with the word of God. I promise you that as you read, your minds will be enlightened and your spirits will be lifted. At first it may seem tedious, but that will change into a wondrous experience with thoughts and words of things divine.

YOUR DIVINE POTENTIAL

Behold thou hast a gift, and blessed art thou
because of thy gift. Remember it is sacred
and cometh from above.

—DOCTRINE AND COVENANTS 6:10

You need never feel inferior. You need never feel that you were born without talents or without opportunities to give them expression. There is something of divinity in you. You have such tremendous potential because of your inherited nature. Every one of you was endowed by your Father in Heaven with a tremendous capacity to do good in the world. Cultivate the art of being kind, of being thoughtful, of being helpful. Refine within you the quality of mercy which comes as a part of the divine attributes you have inherited.

TEACH YOUR CHILDREN TO WORK

For thou shalt eat the labour of thine hands:
happy shalt thou be, and it shall be well with thee.

—PSALM 128:2

Children need to work with their parents—to wash dishes with them, to mop floors with them, to mow lawns, to prune trees and shrubbery, to paint and fix up and clean up and do a hundred other things where they will learn that labor is the price of cleanliness and progress and prosperity.

COUNSEL FOR LEADERS

But rise, and stand upon thy feet: for I have appeared unto thee for this purpose, to make thee a minister and a witness. . .to open their eyes and to turn them from darkness to light.

—ACTS 26:16, 18

It is important for leaders to learn to speak out in a way that is persuasive without being heavy-handed or offensive.

The problem with most of us is that we are afraid to stand up for what we believe, to be witnesses for what is true and right. We want to do the right thing, but we are troubled by fears. So we sit back, and the world drifts about us, and society increasingly adopts attitudes and standards of behavior of which most of us do not approve.

ETERNAL COMPANIONS

Husbands, love your wives, even as Christ also
loved the church, and gave himself for it.

—EPHESIANS 5:25

There is a bond of affection that exists between husbands and wives which makes us know that there is nothing more precious than that companionship which becomes possible only in the house of the Lord. What a wonderful thing it is to be married for time and all eternity. What a precious and marvelous and wonderful thing that is.

A DAUGHTER OF GOD

Favour is deceitful, and beauty is vain: but a
woman that feareth the Lord, she shall be praised.

—PROVERBS 31:30

Of all the creations of the Almighty, there is
none more beautiful, none more inspiring than a
lovely daughter of God who walks in virtue, with
an understanding of why she should do so, who
honors and respects her body as a thing sacred and
divine, who cultivates her mind and constantly
enlarges the horizon of her understanding, who
nurtures her spirit with everlasting truth.

July

*I seek not for honor of the
world, but for the glory
of my God, and the
freedom and welfare
of my country.*

—ALMA 60:36

HAPPINESS IN SERVING

Shall we not go on in so great a cause? Go forward
and not backward. Courage, . . . and on, on to the
victory! Let your hearts rejoice, and be exceedingly
glad. Let the earth break forth into singing. Let the
dead speak forth anthems of eternal praise to the
King Immanuel, who hath ordained, before the world
was, that which would enable us to redeem them out
of their prison; for the prisoners shall go free.

—DOCTRINE AND COVENANTS 128:22

Do you want to be happy? Forget yourself and
get lost in this great cause. Lend your efforts to
helping people. Cultivate a spirit of forgiveness in
your heart against any who might have offended
you. Look to the Lord and live and work to lift and
serve His sons and daughters. You will come to
know a happiness that you have never known
before if you will do that.

ACKNOWLEDGING GOD

Before destruction the heart of man is haughty,
and before honour is humility.

—PROVERBS 18:12

It is acknowledgment of the Almighty that gives civility and refinement to our actions. It is accountability to Him that brings discipline into our lives. It is gratitude for His gracious favors that takes from us the arrogance to which we are so prone.

THE SUSTAINING POWER OF PRAYER

After I had retired to my bed for the night, I betook myself to prayer and supplication to Almighty God for forgiveness of all my sins and follies, and also for a manifestation to me, that I might know of my state and standing before him; for I had full confidence in obtaining a divine manifestation, as I previously had one.

—JOSEPH SMITH–HISTORY 1:29

Believe in the power of prayer. Believe in getting on your knees every morning and every night and talking with your Father in Heaven concerning the feelings of your hearts, and the desires of your minds in righteousness. There is no power upon the earth like the power of prayer.

A CHOICE LAND

Behold, this is a choice land, and whatsoever nation
shall possess it shall be free from bondage, and from
captivity, and from all other nations under
heaven, if they will but serve the God
of the land, who is Jesus Christ.

—ETHER 2:12

I marvel at the miracle of America, the land which the God of Heaven long ago declared to be a land choice above all other lands.

I love America for her great and brawny strength, I love her for her generous heart. I love her for her tremendous spiritual strengths. She is unique among the nations of the earth—in her discovery, in her birth as a nation, in the amalgamation of the races that have come to her shores, in the strength of her government, in the goodness of her people.

God bless America, for she is His creation.

USE YOUR TALENTS TO BLESS OTHERS

For unto every one who hath obtained other
talents, shall be given, and he shall have in
abundance. But from him that hath not
obtained other talents, shall be taken
away even that which he hath received.

—JST, MATTHEW 25:29–30

I do not have to be a scrub, though my work may be menial. Though my contribution may be small, I can perform it with dignity and offer it with unselfishness. My talents may not be great, but I can use them to bless the lives of others.

WALK HUMBLY

Put your trust in that Spirit which leadeth to do
good—yea, to do justly, to walk humbly.

–DOCTRINE AND COVENANTS 11:12

Be humble. There is no place for arrogance in
our lives. There is no place for conceit in our lives.
There is no place for egotism in our lives. We have
work to do. We have things to accomplish.

TEACH SELF-RELIANCE

Think of your brethren like unto yourselves, and be
familiar with all and free with your substance,
that they may be rich like unto you.

—JACOB 2:17

Where there is poverty among our people, we must do all we can to help them to lift themselves, to establish their lives upon a foundation of self-reliance that can come of training. Education is the key to opportunity. It is our solemn obligation, it is our certain responsibility to help others become self-reliant and successful. I believe the Lord does not wish to see His people condemned to live in poverty. I believe He would have the faithful enjoy the good things of the earth. He would have us do all we can to help one another toward this end. And He will bless us as we do so.

BLESSINGS IN ABUNDANCE

I call heaven and earth to record this day against
you, that I have set before you life and death,
blessing and cursing: therefore choose life,
that both thou and thy seed may live.

—DEUTERONOMY 30:19

May the heavens open, and may blessings come
down upon you in abundance as you walk in faithfulness before the Lord.

LISTEN TO THE SPIRIT

Yea, behold, I will tell you in your mind and in your heart, by the Holy Ghost, which shall come upon you and which shall dwell in your heart. Now, behold, this is the spirit of revelation; behold, this is the spirit by which Moses brought the children of Israel through the Red Sea on dry ground. Therefore this is thy gift; apply unto it, and blessed art thou, for it shall deliver you out of the hands of your enemies, when, if it were not so, they would slay you and bring your soul to destruction.

Oh, remember these words, and keep my commandments. Remember, this is your gift.

—DOCTRINE AND COVENANTS 8:2–5

Listen to the whisperings of the Spirit, the gift of revelation to which you are entitled.

SEEK ETERNAL TRUTHS

Wherefore, seek not the things of this world but seek
ye first to build up the kingdom of God, and to
establish his righteousness, and all these
things shall be added unto you.

—JST, MATTHEW 6:38

Seek for the real things, not the artificial. Seek for the everlasting truths, not the passing whim. Seek for the eternal things of God, not for that which is here today, gone tomorrow. Look to God and live, as the scripture enjoins us.

INNER STRENGTH

For God hath not given us the spirit of fear;
but of power, and of love, and of a sound mind.

—2 TIMOTHY 1:7

God hath not given you the spirit of fear. That comes from the adversary. The Lord has given you the power of love, and a sound mind; the power of the priesthood, the power of your call, love for the gospel which you teach, for the people you teach, and for the Lord.

PRIORITIES

*And see that all these things are done in wisdom
and order; for it is not requisite that a man should
run faster than he has strength. And again, it is
expedient that he should be diligent, that thereby he
might win the prize; therefore, all things
must be done in order.*

—MOSIAH 4:27

Just take things one day at a time, otherwise you'll
be overwhelmed.

OBSERVE THE SABBATH

If thou turn away thy foot from the sabbath, from
doing thy pleasure on my holy day; and call the
sabbath a delight, the holy of the Lord, honourable;
and shalt honour him, not doing thine own ways,
nor finding thine own pleasure, nor speaking thine
own words: Then shalt thou delight thyself in
the Lord; and I will cause thee to ride upon the
high places of the earth, and feed thee with
the heritage of Jacob thy father: for the
mouth of the Lord hath spoken it.

—ISAIAH 58:13–14

If you have any doubt about the wisdom, the divinity of observing the Sabbath day, stay at home and gather your family about you, teach them the gospel, enjoy yourselves together on the Sabbath day, come to your meetings, participate. You will know that the principle of the Sabbath is a true principle which brings with it great blessings.

A CALL TO ACTION

Therefore to him that knoweth to do good,
and doeth it not, to him it is sin.

—JAMES 4:17

You can't plow a field simply by turning it over in your mind.

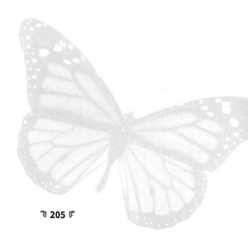

A Believing Heart

Believe in God; believe that he is, and that he
created all things, both in heaven and in earth;
believe that he has all wisdom, and all power,
both in heaven and in earth.

—MOSIAH 4:9

Be not faithless, but believing" (John 20:27). Believing in what? Believing in God our Eternal Father, as the Father of our spirits, as our leader, as our king. Believing in the Lord, Jesus Christ, our Redeemer, our Savior, our Lord. Cultivate in your hearts a living and vibrant testimony of the restoration of the gospel. Believe in the Book of Mormon. Be not faithless in the knowledge that the priesthood of God has been restored to the earth. Believe in goodness. Believe in yourselves. Believe that each of you is a child of God with a divine birthright.

GIVE LOVING SERVICE

Yea, and now behold, O my son, the Lord doth
give me exceedingly great joy in the
fruit of my labors.

—ALMA 36:25

Tremendous happiness and peace of mind are the results of loving service to others. Nobody can live fully and happily who lives only unto himself or herself.

WALK IN VIRTUE

*Be careful for nothing; but in every thing by prayer
and supplication with thanksgiving let your
requests be made known unto God. And the peace
of God, which passeth all understanding,
shall keep your hearts and minds
through Christ Jesus.*

—PHILIPPIANS 4:6–7

The peace of conscience that flows from personal virtue is the only personal peace that is not counterfeit. And beyond all of this is the unfailing promise of God to those who walk in virtue, "exceeding great and precious promises: that by these ye might be partakers of the divine nature" (2 Peter 1:4).

THE SUSTAINING POWER OF LOVE

Behold, I speak with boldness,
having authority from God;
and I fear not what man can do;
for perfect love casteth out all fear.

—MORONI 8:16

There is nothing as energizing, as confidence-building, as sustaining as the power of love. How substantial is its influence on the human mind and heart! How great and magnificent is its power in overcoming fear and doubt, worry and discouragement!

FIRST PRAYER, THEN ACTION

And after I, Enos, had heard these words, my faith
began to be unshaken in the Lord; and I prayed
unto him with many long strugglings for my
brethren, the Lamanites. And it came to pass that
after I had prayed and labored with all diligence,
the Lord said unto me: I will grant unto thee
according to thy desires, because of thy faith.

—ENOS 1:11–12

We get on our knees and we ask the Lord to help us live in obedience to His commandments. We get on our feet and resolve to be better people than we were when we knelt down. Our beliefs will govern our actions. God help us to be those who are not faithless, but believing.

MISSIONARIES SERVE WITH FAITH

*And I give unto them a commandment that they
shall go forth for a little season, and it shall be given
by the power of the Spirit when they shall return.
And ye shall go forth in the power of my Spirit,
preaching my gospel, two by two, in my name, lifting
up your voices as with the sound of a trump,
declaring my word like unto angels of God. And ye
shall go forth baptizing with water, saying: Repent
ye, repent ye, for the kingdom of heaven is at hand.*

—DOCTRINE AND COVENANTS 42:5–7

Shining through all missionary service is the
reassuring faith that the work is true and that the
service being given is given unto God. Missionaries
serve with faith in their hearts. It is a phenomenon
of great power that quietly whispers, "This cause is
true, and to you there is an obligation to serve
regardless of the cost."

SERVICE IN THE CHURCH

Wherefore, now let every man learn his duty,
and to act in the office in which he is
appointed, in all diligence.
—DOCTRINE AND COVENANTS 107:99

Let the Church be your dear friend. Let it be your great companion. Serve wherever you are called to serve. Do what you are asked to do. Every position you hold will add to your capacity. Every bit of service will bring its own reward. You will serve in many capacities before your lives are complete. Some of them may seem small, but there is no small or unimportant calling in this Church. Every calling is important.

RESPECT ONE ANOTHER

And it came to pass that there was no contention in the land, because of the love of God which did dwell in the hearts of the people.

—4 NEPHI 1:15

I do not like labels; I do not like to categorize people. We are all individuals—men and women, sons and daughters of God, not a mass of "look-alikes" or "do-alikes." All of us are very much alike in our capacity to think, to reason, to be miserable, if you please; in our need to be happy, to love and be loved. We are subject to the same pains, the same sensitivities, the same emotions. We are all individuals living together, hopefully with respect for one another, notwithstanding our unique personal situations.

SPIRITUAL EXPERIENCES

And we ask thee, Holy Father, that thy servants may go forth from this house armed with thy power, and that thy name may be upon them, and thy glory be round about them, and thine angels have charge over them; And from this place they may bear exceedingly great and glorious tidings, in truth, unto the ends of the earth, that they may know that this is thy work, and that thou hast put forth thy hand, to fulfil that which thou hast spoken by the mouths of the prophets, concerning the last days.

—DOCTRINE AND COVENANTS 109:22–23

The older I grow the less concerned I become with quotas and statistics and percentages, and the more I become concerned with the kind of experience that the soul of man has in the Lord's church, and particularly in the Lord's holy temple.

GOSPEL PIONEERS

The path of the just is as the shining light.

—PROVERBS 4:18

It is good to look to the past to gain appreciation for the present and perspective for the future. It is good to look upon the virtues of those who have gone before, to gain strength for whatever lies ahead. It is good to reflect upon the work of those who labored so hard and gained so little in this world, but one of whose dreams and early plans, so well nurtured, has come a great harvest of which we are the beneficiaries. Their tremendous example can become a compelling motivation for us all, for each of us is a pioneer in his own life, often in his own family, and many of us pioneer daily in trying to establish a gospel foothold in distant parts of the world.

OUR PIONEER LEGACY

But as it is written, Eye hath not seen, nor ear
heard, neither have entered into the heart
of man, the things which God hath
prepared for them that love him.

—1 CORINTHIANS 2:9

The future is ahead. As great things were expected of the pioneers, so are they of us. We note what they did with what they had. We have so much more, with an overwhelming challenge to go on and build the kingdom of God. We are engaged in a great consuming crusade for truth and goodness.

THE LAW OF THE HARVEST

Hearken, O ye who have given your names to go
forth to proclaim my gospel, and to prune my
vineyard. Behold, I say unto you that it is my
will that you should go forth and not tarry.

—DOCTRINE AND COVENANTS 75:2–3

There must be labor, incessant and constant, if
there is to be a harvest.

Lift and Help Others

Depart from evil, and do good;
seek peace, and pursue it.

—PSALM 34:14

I do not care how old you are, how young you are, whatever. You can lift people and help them. Heaven knows there are so very, very, very many people in this world who need help. Oh, so very, very many. Let's get the cankering, selfish attitude out of our lives and stand a little taller and reach a little higher in the service of others. As Browning said, "A man's reach should exceed his grasp." Stand taller, stand higher, lift those with feeble knees, hold up the arms of those that hang down. Live the gospel of Jesus Christ. Forget yourself.

For the Salvation of Souls

For behold, this is my work and my glory—
to bring to pass the immortality
and eternal life of man.

—MOSES 1:39

I invite you to look beyond the narrow boundaries of your own wards and rise to the larger vision of this, the work of God. We have a challenge to meet, a work to do beyond the comprehension of any of us—that is, to assist our Heavenly Father to save His sons and daughters of all generations, both the living and the dead, to work for the salvation not only of those in the Church, but for those presently outside, wherever they may be. No body of people on the face of the earth has received a stronger mandate from the God of heaven than have we of this Church.

THE SPOILS OF PERSONAL DEBT

Go, sell the oil, and pay thy debt,
and live thou and thy children of the rest.

—2 KINGS 4:7

I have seen in a very vivid way the terrible tragedies of many who have gone on a binge of borrowing for things they really do not need. How many people might have been saved pain and misery, suffering, embarrassment, and trouble had they listened to counsel concerning personal debt.

OPPOSITION

*And Eve, his wife, heard all these things and was
glad, saying: Were it not for our transgression we
never should have had seed, and never should
have known good and evil, and the joy of our
redemption, and the eternal life which
God giveth unto all the obedient.*

—MOSES 5:11

The valleys of discouragement make more beautiful the peaks of achievement.

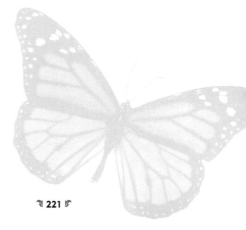

A GREAT SEASON IN TIME

And it shall come to pass in the last days, saith
God, I will pour out of my Spirit upon all flesh: and
your sons and your daughters shall prophesy, and
your young men shall see visions, and your
old men shall dream dreams: . . . And it
shall come to pass, that whosoever shall
call on the name of the Lord shall be saved.

—ACTS 2:17, 21

How marvelous to be alive at this time—the dawning of the third millennium since the birth of Christ. This is the great summing-up season of the work of the Lord. This is the day of prophecy fulfilled.

AUGUST

*And ye shall know the
truth, and the truth
shall make you free.*

—JOHN 8:32

TEACH SERVICE BY EXAMPLE

Teach them to walk in the ways of truth and
soberness; . . . teach them to love one another,
and to serve one another.

—MOSIAH 4:15

The antidote for selfishness is service, a reaching out to those about us—those in the home and those beyond the walls of the home. A child who grows up in a home where there is a selfish, grasping father or mother is likely to develop those tendencies in his own life. On the other hand, a child who sees his father and mother forgo comforts for themselves as they reach out to those in distress, will likely follow the same pattern when he or she grows to maturity.

Everyday Accomplishments

Wherefore, be not weary in well-doing, for ye are
laying the foundation of a great work. And out of
small things proceedeth that which is great. Behold,
the Lord requireth the heart and a willing mind;
and the willing and obedient shall eat the good
of the land of Zion in these last days.

—DOCTRINE AND COVENANTS 64:33–34

The major work of the world is not done by geniuses. It is done by ordinary people who have learned to work in an extraordinary manner.

LIVE THE GOSPEL

Search diligently, pray always, and be believing,
and all things shall work together for your good, if
ye walk uprightly and remember the covenant
wherewith ye have covenanted one with another.

—DOCTRINE AND COVENANTS 90:24

If you will live the gospel, nearly everything else
will eventually take care of itself.

AN HONEST TITHE

And after that, those who have thus been tithed
shall pay one-tenth of all their interest annually;
and this shall be a standing law unto them forever,
for my holy priesthood, saith the Lord.

—DOCTRINE AND COVENANTS 119:4

Live honestly with the Lord in the payment of tithes and offerings. Tithing is an opportunity to prove our faithfulness. It doesn't take money to pay tithing. It takes faith.

HOME AND FAMILY

And they shall also teach their children to pray,
and to walk uprightly before the Lord.

—DOCTRINE AND COVENANTS 68:28

Every child is entitled to grow up in a home where there is warm and secure companionship, where there is love in the family relationship, where appreciation one for another is taught and exemplified, and where God is acknowledged and His peace and blessings invoked before the family altar.

EXERCISE YOUR FAITH

Therefore may God grant unto you, my brethren,
that ye may begin to exercise your faith unto
repentance, that ye begin to call upon his holy
name, that he would have mercy upon you.

—ALMA 34:17

If you get on your knees and ask for help, and then get up and go to work, you'll be able to find your way through almost any situation.

Magnifying the Priesthood

*And they shall look to the poor and the needy, and
administer to their relief that they shall not suffer;
and send them forth to the place which I
have commanded them.*

—DOCTRINE AND COVENANTS 38:35

Each of us is responsible for the welfare and the growth and development of others. We do not live only unto ourselves. As we serve with diligence, as we teach with faith and testimony, as we lift and strengthen and build convictions of righteousness in those lives we touch, we magnify our priesthood. To live only unto ourselves, on the other hand, to serve grudgingly, to give less than our best effort to our duty, diminishes our priesthood just as looking through the wrong lenses of binoculars reduces the image and makes more distant the object.

PRIESTHOOD STEWARDSHIP

It is required of the Lord, at the hand of every
steward, to render an account of his stewardship,
both in time and in eternity. For he who is faithful
and wise in time is accounted worthy to inherit the
mansions prepared for him of my Father.

—DOCTRINE AND COVENANTS 72:3–4

It is a tremendously humbling experience to realize that the Melchizedek Priesthood which we hold is after the order of the Son of God, and that we have responsibility and accountability to Him and our Eternal Father for all that we do in exercising the stewardship given us.

APPROPRIATE SPEECH

Only let your conversation be as it becometh the gospel of Christ: that whether I come and see you, or else be absent, I may hear of your affairs, that ye stand fast in one spirit, with one mind striving together for the faith of the gospel.

—PHILIPPIANS 1:27

In our dialogues with others we must be an example of the believer. Conversation is the substance of friendly social activity. It can be happy. It can be light. It can be earnest. It can be funny. But it must not be salty, or uncouth, or foul if one is in sincerity a believer in Christ.

"REVERENCE MY SANCTUARY"

Ye shall keep my sabbaths,
and reverence my sanctuary.

—LEVITICUS 19:30

The Lord said, "Draw not nigh hither: put off thy shoes from off thy feet, for the place whereon thou standest is holy ground" (Exodus 3:5). We do not ask our people to remove their shoes when they come into the chapel. But all who come into the Lord's house should have a feeling that they are walking and standing on holy ground and that it becomes them to deport themselves accordingly.

THE BOOK OF MORMON

And the Book of Mormon and the holy scriptures
are given of me for your instruction; and the
power of my Spirit quickeneth all things.

—DOCTRINE AND COVENANTS 33:16

Believe in the Book of Mormon, as another witness of the Son of God. This book has come forth as an added testimony to the world, of the great truths concerning the Master set forth in the Bible. The Bible is the testament of the Old World. The Book of Mormon is the testament of the New World, and they go hand in hand in testimony of the Lord Jesus Christ. This marvelous book of inspiration affirms the validity and the truth of the divine nature of the Son of God. God be thanked for this precious and wonderful testimony. Let us read it. Let us dwell upon its truths. Let us learn its message and be blessed accordingly.

MEMBER MISSIONARIES

Nevertheless, the people of the church did have great joy because of the conversion of the Lamanites, yea, because of the church of God, which had been established among them. And they did fellowship one with another, and did rejoice one with another, and did have great joy.

—HELAMAN 6:3

Bring people into the Church. Bring them in with love. Bring them in with kindness. Bring them in with the example of your lives. So live the gospel that they will see in you something of wonder and beauty and be encouraged to inquire, study the gospel, and join the Church.

DEADLY RUBBISH

And he that looketh upon a woman to lust after her
shall deny the faith, and shall not have the Spirit;
and if he repents not he shall be cast out.

—DOCTRINE AND COVENANTS 42:23

Pornography robs its victims of self-respect and of an appreciation of the beauties of life. It tears down those who indulge and pulls them into a slough of evil thoughts and possibly evil deeds. It seduces, destroys, and distorts the truth about love. It is more deadly than a foul disease. Not one of us can afford to partake of this rubbish. We cannot risk the effect it will have on our spirit and soul. Avoid it like the deadliest of plagues.

ABIDING LOVE

*Love one another: for he that loveth
another hath fulfilled the law.*

—ROMANS 13:8

In a changing world, love can be a constant. It is something that, when sincere, never moves. It is the very essence of the teachings of Christ. It is the security of the home. It is the safeguard of community life. It is a beacon of hope in a world of distress.

CIVILITY IS A VIRTUE

Above all these things put on charity,
which is the bond of perfectness.

—COLOSSIANS 3:14

Caring for others, seeing and reaching beyond our own wants and comforts, cultivating kindness and gentility towards others from all of life's situations and circumstances—these are of the essence of civility, a virtue to be admired, a virtue to be acquired.

FAITH REASSURES

And the work of righteousness shall be peace;
and the effect of righteousness quietness
and assurance for ever.

—ISAIAH 32:17

When doubts arise, when tragedies strike, the quiet voice of faith is heard in the stillness of the night as certain and reassuring as the polar star in the heavens above.

ANSWERS TO PRAYER

*And whoso receiveth you, there I will be also, for I
will go before your face. I will be on your right
hand and on your left, and my Spirit shall
be in your hearts, and mine angels round
about you, to bear you up.*

—DOCTRINE AND COVENANTS 84:88

Sometimes you pray to the Lord with great
earnestness for help, for relief from your struggles.
You wonder why your prayers are not answered as
you would like them to be. We have all had that
experience. But we come to know as the years pass
that our Father in Heaven does hear our prayers.
His wisdom is greater than ours, and we come to
know that He answers our prayers even though the
answers at times are difficult to discern.

LINE UPON LINE

*I will give unto the children of men line upon line
. . . for unto him that receiveth I will give more.*

—2 NEPHI 28:30

Make room for the Church in your life. Let your knowledge of its doctrine grow. Let your understanding of its organization increase. Let your love for its eternal truths become ever and ever stronger.

A REMEDY FOR LONELINESS

Wherefore, be faithful; . . . succor the weak,
lift up the hands which hang down, and
strengthen the feeble knees.

—DOCTRINE AND COVENANTS 81:5

I believe that for most of us the best medicine for loneliness is work and service in behalf of others. I do not wish to minimize your problems, but I do not hesitate to say that there are many others whose problems are more serious than yours. Reach out to serve them, to help them, to encourage them. There are so many boys and girls who fail in school for want of a little personal attention and encouragement. There are so many elderly people who live in misery and loneliness and fear for whom a simple conversation would bring a measure of hope and brightness.

ESTEEM FOR OTHERS

*Therefore, strengthen your brethren in all your
conversation, in all your prayers, in all your
exhortations, and in all your doings.*

—DOCTRINE AND COVENANTS 108:7

Do not indulge in put-downs, in pessimism, in
self-recrimination. Never make fun at the expense
of another. Look for virtue in the lives of all with
whom you associate.

DEVOTION TO CHURCH

*Behold, they have been sent to preach my gospel
among the congregations of the wicked; wherefore,
I give unto them a commandment, thus: Thou
shalt not idle away thy time, neither shalt thou
bury thy talent that it may not be known.*

—DOCTRINE AND COVENANTS 60:13

The Church needs your strength. It needs your love and loyalty and devotion. It needs a little more of your time and energy. I am not asking anyone to give more at the expense of his or her employer or at the expense of his or her family. But I am suggesting that we spend a little less time in idleness, in the fruitless pursuit of watching some inane and empty television programs. Time so utilized can be put to better advantage, and the consequences will be wonderful.

Self-Improvement

And all this for the benefit of the church of the living God, that every man may improve upon his talent, that every man may gain other talents, yea, even an hundred fold, to be cast into the Lord's storehouse, to become the common property of the whole church.

—DOCTRINE AND COVENANTS 82:18

We can improve, and when all is said and done that's what this is all about: improvement, changing our lives so that we can help people change their lives and be better; building Zion on the earth.

ENCOURAGEMENT

For I was an hungred, and ye gave me meat:
I was thirsty, and ye gave me drink: I was a
stranger, and ye took me in: Naked, and ye
clothed me: I was sick, and ye visited me:
I was in prison, and ye came unto me.

—MATTHEW 25:35–36

All of us can become discouraged. It is important to know, when you feel down, that many others do also and that their circumstances are often much worse than ours. And it is important to know that when one of us is down, it becomes the obligation of his friends to give him a lift.

BLESSINGS OF TEMPLE ATTENDANCE

One thing have I desired of the Lord, that will I seek
after; that I may dwell in the house of the Lord all
the days of my life, to behold the beauty of the Lord,
and to enquire in his temple. For in the time of
trouble he shall hide me in his pavilion: in the secret
of his tabernacle shall he hide me;
he shall set me up upon a rock.

—PSALM 27:4–5

If you are geographically able, go to the temple on a regular basis. You will be better fathers and husbands, better wives and mothers. I know your lives are busy. I know that you have much to do. But I make you a promise that if you will go to the house of the Lord, you will be blessed; life will be better for you.

THE JOY OF PARENTHOOD

*I have no greater joy than to hear that
my children walk in truth.*

—3 JOHN 1:4

Of all the joys of life, none other equals that of happy parenthood. Of all the responsibilities with which we struggle, none other is so serious. To rear children in an atmosphere of love, security, and faith is the most rewarding of all challenges. The good result from such efforts becomes life's most satisfying compensation.

TEACHING WITH THE SPIRIT

Wherefore, I the Lord ask you this question—
unto what were ye ordained? To preach my
gospel by the Spirit, even the Comforter
which was sent forth to teach the truth.

—DOCTRINE AND COVENANTS 50:13–14

We need to do a more thorough job in the teaching process to get the Spirit down into the hearts of those we teach. It is more than intellectual; it is more than a mental assessment. It must be a thing of the heart, a thing of the Spirit.

A Covenant People

But ye are a chosen generation,
a royal priesthood, an holy nation,
a peculiar people.

—1 PETER 2:9

We are a covenant people and great are the obligations which go with that covenant. We cannot be ordinary people. We must rise above the crowd. We must stand a little taller. We must be a little better, a little kinder, a little more generous, a little more courteous, a little more thoughtful, a little more outreaching to others.

A GOOD TEACHER

And as all have not faith, seek ye diligently
and teach one another words of wisdom.

—DOCTRINE AND COVENANTS 109:7

There is an immortality in ideas and inspiration
that a good teacher imparts to a receptive student,
who in turn imparts to those who follow after him.

The First Vision

For I had seen a vision; I knew it, and I knew that
God knew it, and I could not deny it,
neither dared I do it.

—JOSEPH SMITH–HISTORY 1:25

You cannot build strength on falsehood. You cannot build conviction on imagination. The basis of this great thing which we have, the restored gospel of the Lord Jesus Christ and the Church, which was organized under divine authority, finds its roots in the vision which occurred in a quiet grove in upstate New York. It is rooted in the certainty of Joseph Smith's undeniable experience.

RESPECT FOR OTHERS

Let brotherly love continue.

—HEBREWS 13:1

Work with respect for your associates, for their opinions, for their beliefs, with appreciation for their problems, and with a desire to help them should they stumble.

A City Set upon a Hill

I give unto you to be the light of this people.
A city that is set on a hill cannot be hid.

—3 NEPHI 12:14

We are all in this together. Every man, woman, and child who belongs to this Church is part of this movement. Let us work and accomplish and become as a city set upon a hill whose light cannot be hid from the world.

SEPTEMBER

*Blessed are all they that
put their trust in him.*

—PSALM 2:12

Sons and Daughters of God

Beloved, now are we the sons of God, and it doth not yet appear what we shall be: but we know that, when he shall appear, we shall be like him; for we shall see him as he is.

—1 JOHN 3:2

You and I are sons and daughters of God, with something of divinity within us. Let us stand tall, my brothers and sisters. Let us live the gospel. Let us be busy in the church. Let us learn of its doctrine. Let us feed upon its teachings. Let us grow in faith and faithfulness before the world.

INDIVIDUAL PROGRESS

And be not conformed to this world: but be ye
transformed by the renewing of your mind,
that ye may prove what is that good, and
acceptable, and perfect, will of God.

—ROMANS 12:2

Hopefully, we're making some progress in our own individual lives. I hope that every person can feel he or she is a little better today than they were yesterday, a little kinder, a little more gracious, a little more generous, a little more honest in purpose and word and deed, a little stronger for the right, a little stronger to resist the wrong.

STRENGTHENED BY FAITH

Now, we will compare the word unto a seed. Now, if
ye give place, that a seed may be planted in your
heart, behold, if it be a true seed, or a good seed,
if ye do not cast it out by your unbelief, that ye
will resist the Spirit of the Lord, behold, it will
begin to swell within your breasts; and when
you feel these swelling motions, ye will begin to
say within yourselves—It must needs be that
this is a good seed, or that the word is good,
for it beginneth to enlarge my soul; yea,
it beginneth to enlighten my understanding,
yea, it beginneth to be delicious to me.

—ALMA 32:28

The faith to try leads to direction by the Spirit,
and the fruits that flow therefrom are marvelous to
behold and experience.

THE QUALITY OF MERCY

Blessed are the merciful:
for they shall obtain mercy.

—MATTHEW 5:7

There is so much of hatred in the world. There is so much of bitterness in the world. There is so much of selfishness in the world. There is so much of arrogance in the world. What a marvelous thing to have in our lives the quality of mercy, of reaching out to others in a spirit of mercy, love, and kindness.

TEMPLE WORTHINESS

*Depart ye, depart ye, go ye out from thence, touch
no unclean thing; go ye out of the midst of her; be
ye clean, that bear the vessels of the Lord.*

—ISAIAH 52:11

Each of us has an obligation to see that the
temple is kept sacred and free of any defilement—
first, as to our own personal worthiness, and
second, as to the worthiness of those whom we
may encourage or assist in going to the house of
the Lord.

MAKE TIME FOR PERSONAL REFLECTION

Therefore, let your hearts be comforted concerning Zion; for all flesh is in mine hands; be still and know that I am God.

—DOCTRINE AND COVENANTS 101:16

Our lives become extremely busy. We run from one thing to another. We wear ourselves out in thoughtless pursuit of goals which are largely ephemeral. We are entitled to spend some time with ourselves in introspection, in development, in thinking, meditating, pondering things.

Sabbath Activities

Six days shalt thou labour, and do all thy work:
But the seventh day is the sabbath of the Lord
thy God: in it thou shalt not do any work.

—EXODUS 20:9–10

Keep the Sabbath day holy. You do not have to shop on Sunday. Let this day be a day of meditation, of reading the scriptures, of talking with your families, and of dwelling on the things of God. If you do so you will be blessed.

ENJOY LIFE

A merry heart doeth good like a medicine:
but a broken spirit drieth the bones.

—PROVERBS 17:22

In all of living have much fun and laughter. Life is
to be enjoyed, not just endured.

ENDURE TO THE END

He that endureth to the end shall be saved.

—MATTHEW 10:22

Walk with integrity; in storm and sunshine, be faithful; in richness or in poverty, be faithful; in youth or old age, be faithful. Hold out until the end and God will bless you and crown your days with sweetness, and peace, and love.

THE VALUE OF CHILDREN

Children are an heritage of the Lord.

—PSALM 127:3

Children are the promise of the future, the assurance of greater things to come.

COMMIT TO YOUR EDUCATION

Teach ye diligently . . . that you may be instructed more perfectly in theory, in principle, in doctrine, in the law of the gospel, in all things that pertain unto the kingdom of God, . . . Of things both in heaven and in the earth, and under the earth; things which have been, things which are, things which must shortly come to pass; things which are at home, things which are abroad; the wars and the perplexities of the nations, and the judgments which are on the land; and a knowledge also of countries and of kingdoms.

—DOCTRINE AND COVENANTS 88:78–79

This is a competitive world. You need all the education you can get. The Lord wants you to educate your mind and your heart. It does not matter what field you choose, but become a workman of integrity, prepared to contribute to the world.

AGE IS RELATIVE

They shall still bring forth fruit in old age;
they shall be fat and flourishing.

—PSALM 92:14

Age is more a matter of how you feel, how you think, and what's going on in your head than what's going on in your feet.

PREPARE FOR A CAREER

Apply thine heart unto instruction,
and thine ears to the words of knowledge.

—PROVERBS 23:12

I don't care what you plan to do as your life's vocation, but prepare yourselves. Get the best education you can. Qualify yourselves in the best way you know how. It's part of a mandate from the Lord that you train yourselves.

THE POWER OF LOVE

Herein is love, not that we loved God, but that
he loved us, and sent his Son to be the
propitiation for our sins.

—1 JOHN 4:10

There is nothing as energizing, as confidence-building, as sustaining as the power of love.

BELIEVE IN JESUS CHRIST

Who is he that overcometh the world,
but he that believeth that Jesus is the Son of God?

—1 JOHN 5:5

Believe in Jesus Christ, our Savior and our Redeemer, the Son of God, who came to earth and walked the dusty roads of Palestine—the Son of God—to teach us the way of truth and light and salvation, and who, in one great and glorious act offered an atonement for each of us. He opened the way of salvation and exaltation for us, under which we may go forward in the Church and kingdom of God. Be not faithless, but believe in the great and wonderful and marvelous blessings of the Atonement.

LEADERSHIP REQUIRES HONESTY

And they were among the people of Nephi, and also
numbered among the people who were of the church
of God. And they were also distinguished
for their zeal towards God, and also towards men;
for they were perfectly honest and upright
in all things; and they were firm in the faith
of Christ, even unto the end.

—ALMA 27:27

Leadership—of the family, an organization, our society, or even the nation—erodes and eventually falls apart without honesty and integrity. Honesty is the keystone that holds any organization together.

CIVILITY AND THE GOLDEN RULE

All things whatsoever ye would that men
should do to you, do ye even so to them.
—MATTHEW 7:12

Civility, I submit, is what gives savor to our lives. It is the salt that speaks of good taste, good manners, good breeding. It becomes an expression of the Golden Rule. Civility covers a host of matters in how one human being relates to another with basic human kindness and goodness. Civility requires us to restrain and control ourselves, and at the same time to act with respect towards others.

FORGIVENESS

For the wages of sin is death; but the gift of God is eternal life through Jesus Christ our Lord.

—ROMANS 6:23

If you have made a mistake, if you have become involved in any immoral behavior, all is not lost. Memory of that mistake will likely linger, but the deed can be forgiven, and you can rise above the past to live a life fully acceptable unto the Lord where there has been repentance. He has promised that He will forgive our sins and remember them no more against us.

EVIDENCE OF FAITH

And now, I, Moroni, would speak somewhat
concerning these things; I would show unto
the world that faith is things which are hoped
for and not seen; wherefore, dispute not
because ye see not, for ye receive no witness
until after the trial of your faith.

—ETHER 12:6

I t is faith that is the converter. It is faith that is the teacher. This precious and marvelous gift of faith, this gift from God our Eternal Father is the strength of this work and the quiet vibrancy of its message. Faith underlies it all. Faith is the substance of it all. Whether it be going into the mission field, living the Word of Wisdom, paying one's tithing, it is all the same. It is the faith within us that is evidenced in all we do.

PURSUE A WORTHY VOCATION

Learn wisdom in thy youth.

—ALMA 37:35

Find purpose in your life. During your young adult years choose the things that you would like to do, and educate yourselves to be effective in their pursuit. It is very difficult to settle on a vocation, but you need the means and skills by which to earn a living. Study your options. Pray to the Lord earnestly for direction. Then pursue your course with resolution.

Unity Felt through the Spirit

For ye are all the children of God by faith in Christ
Jesus. For as many of you as have been baptized
into Christ have put on Christ. There is neither
Jew nor Greek, there is neither bond nor free,
there is neither male nor female: for ye are
all one in Christ Jesus.

—GALATIANS 3:26–28

There is universal appeal in the gospel of Jesus Christ. We come from different parts of the world, we come out of a variety of cultures, but we are all sons and daughters of God, and when we listen, when we place ourselves in tune with His Holy Spirit, there is a response within our hearts that is similar, and we feel it. Each of us has felt it in our lives. And regardless of the source, we all respond in the same way. We "speak in the name of God the Lord, even the Savior of the world" (D&C 1:20).

THE WORK ROLLS FORTH

From thence shall the gospel roll forth unto the ends
of the earth, as the stone which is cut out of the
mountain without hands shall roll forth,
until it has filled the whole earth.

—DOCTRINE AND COVENANTS 65:2

This work stands as an anchor of stability, an anchor of values, in a world whose values are shifting. We stand for something. Our values find their roots in the teachings of the gospel of Jesus Christ. These are unchanging. They are today as they were when Jesus walked the roads of Palestine. They are as applicable now as they were then. They have been tested in the cauldron of human history, and they have not been found wanting. We expect great things of our people. This religion is demanding. It requires self-discipline. It requires study and courage and faith.

RISE ABOVE WEAKNESSES

And blessed is he that is found faithful unto my name at the last day, for he shall be lifted up to dwell in the kingdom prepared for him from the foundation of the world.

—ETHER 4:19

Do we have frailties? Yes, of course we do. Do we have members of the Church who are not what they ought to be? Of course we do. Some of them may be your neighbors. You might have one for a roommate. Do not condemn the Church for that. Rather, say to yourself, "My membership in this Church is worth more than all of the evil that people can do to me," if that is what it takes. You be faithful; you be true.

BE A GOOD SAMARITAN

But a certain Samaritan, as he journeyed,
came where he was: and when he saw
him, he had compassion on him.

—LUKE 10:33

There are so many who have been hurt and injured and who need a good Samaritan to bind up their wounds and help them on their way. A small kindness can bring a great blessing to someone in distress and a sweet feeling to the one who befriends him.

SEEK LEARNING

Yea, seek ye out of the best books words of wisdom,
seek learning even by study and also by faith.

—DOCTRINE AND COVENANTS 109:7

I know of no other practice which will make one more attractive in conversation than to be well-read in a variety of subjects. There is a great potential within each of us to go on learning. Regardless of our age, unless there be serious illness, we can read, study, drink in the writings of wonderful men and women. It is never too late to learn.

TEACH FROM THE HEART

Verily I say unto you, he that is ordained of me and sent forth to preach the word of truth by the Comforter, in the Spirit of truth, doth he preach it by the Spirit of truth or some other way? And if it be by some other way it is not of God.

—DOCTRINE AND COVENANTS 50:17–18

Teachers must speak out of their hearts rather than out of their books to communicate their love for the Lord and this precious work, and somehow it will catch fire in the hearts of those they teach.

MORONI'S PROMISE

*And when ye shall receive these things, I would
exhort you that ye would ask God, the Eternal
Father, in the name of Christ, if these things are not
true; and if ye shall ask with a sincere heart, with real
intent, having faith in Christ, he will manifest the
truth of it unto you, by the power of the Holy Ghost.*

—MORONI 10:4–5

I hope that every man and woman and boy and
girl has read the Book of Mormon. I hope you have
pondered its contents. I hope you have prayed
about it if you have any doubt concerning it. I hope
you will read it again, and again, and again. And I
promise you, as Moroni has promised you, that if
you will read the Book of Mormon carefully, and
thoughtfully, and get on your knees and ask the
Lord if it is true, by the power of the Holy Ghost
you will come to know the truth of that book.

KNOWLEDGE REQUIRES EFFORT

You have supposed that I would give it unto you,
when you took no thought save it was to ask me.
But, behold, I say unto you, that you must
study it out in your mind; then you
must ask me if it be right.

—DOCTRINE AND COVENANTS 9:7–8

Knowledge without labor is profitless. Knowledge with labor is genius.

PARTAKE OF TEMPLE BLESSINGS

And when thy people transgress, any of them, they may speedily repent and return unto thee, and find favor in thy sight, and be restored to the blessings which thou hast ordained to be poured out upon those who shall reverence thee in thy house.

—DOCTRINE AND COVENANTS 109:21

The temple is a place of light, a place of peace, a place of love where we deal with the things of eternity. If you are not now worthy to go into that holy house, I urge you to put your life in order so that you may go there and partake of unique and wonderful blessings.

PATRIARCHAL BLESSINGS

For since the beginning of the world have not men heard nor perceived by the ear, neither hath any eye seen, O God, besides thee, how great things thou hast prepared for him that waiteth for thee.

—DOCTRINE AND COVENANTS 133:45

A patriarchal blessing is a unique and sacred and personal and wonderful thing that may be given to every member of this Church who lives worthy of it. All who are mature enough to understand the importance of a patriarchal blessing should receive one.

OCTOBER

*In the strength of the
Lord thou canst
do all things.*

—ALMA 20:4

Be Strong and Faithful

And he said unto the children of men: Follow thou
me. Wherefore, my beloved brethren, can we
follow Jesus save we shall be willing to keep
the commandments of the Father?

—2 NEPHI 31:10

We live at a very interesting time in the history
of the Church. It is a time of great challenges and
great opportunities. Every one of us needs to stand
tall and be strong and faithful and walk in the foot-
steps of the Master. We need to examine our own
lives to see that they radiate the Spirit of the Lord
who taught us the great saving principles of the
gospel.

THE CAUSE OF CHRIST

They who are not for me are
against me, saith our God

—2 NEPHI 10:16

The cause of Christ does not need your doubts; it needs your strength and time and talents; and as you exercise these in service, your faith will grow and your doubts will wane. You need the Church, and the Church needs you. The cause of Christ does not need critics; it needs workers.

CULTIVATE YOUR TESTIMONY

And this is the confidence that we have in him, that,
if we ask any thing according to his will, he heareth
us: And if we know that he hear us, whatsoever
we ask, we know that we have the petitions
that we desired of him.

—1 JOHN 5:14–15

Cultivate a testimony of the restoration of the gospel. You have to nourish, you have to feed your testimony by reading the scriptures, praying, and by being active and faithful in the Church, by doing His will. If you don't have a testimony, go to work to get one. The Lord told us how to do it. He said, "If any man will do his will, he shall know of the doctrine, whether it be of God, or whether I speak of myself" (John 7:17). It is just that simple. It is a law of God that carries with it a marvelous and remarkable promise.

SUSTAINING CHURCH LEADERS

Remember them which have the rule over you, who have spoken unto you the word of God: whose faith follow, considering the end of their conversation.

—HEBREWS 13:7

The procedure of sustaining is much more than a ritualistic raising of the hand. It is a commitment to uphold, to support, to assist those who have been selected.

GO FORWARD WITH FAITH

Now behold, a marvelous work is about to come
forth among the children of men. Therefore,
O ye that embark in the service of God, see
that ye serve him with all your heart,
might, mind and strength, that ye may stand
blameless before God at the last day.

—DOCTRINE AND COVENANTS 4:1–2

These are the best of times in the history of this work. What a wonderful privilege and great responsibility are ours to be an important part of this latter-day work of God. Do not become sidetracked by the wiles of Satan that seem so rampant in our era. Rather, let us go forward with faith and with the vision of the great and marvelous future that lies ahead as this work grows in strength and gains in momentum.

LIVE WORTHY OF GOD'S BLESSINGS

Draw near unto me and I will draw near unto you;
seek me diligently and ye shall find me; ask, and ye
shall receive; knock, and it shall be opened unto
you. Whatsoever ye ask the Father in my name it
shall be given unto you, that is expedient for you.

—DOCTRINE AND COVENANTS 88:63–64

Live so that God may open the windows of heaven and shower down His blessings upon you. Pray to Him. Pray for direction in your lives. Let Him lead you and guide you and help you with the decisions you have to make. Live close to Him. Live graciously one with another.

BE PRAYERFUL

*Confess your faults one to another, and pray one for
another, that ye may be healed. The effectual
fervent prayer of a righteous man availeth much.*

—JAMES 5:16

Prayer unlocks the powers of heaven in our
behalf. Prayer is the great gift which our Eternal
Father has given us by which we may approach
Him and speak with Him in the name of the Lord
Jesus Christ. Be prayerful. You cannot make it
alone. You cannot reach your potential alone. You
need the help of the Lord.

TOUCH OTHERS' LIVES

Ye are the light of the world.

—MATTHEW 5:14

No man or woman proceeds alone. All of us are largely the products of the lives which touch upon our lives.

JOY IN FOLLOWING CHRIST

Therefore, what manner of men ought ye to be?
Verily I say unto you, even as I am.

—3 NEPHI 27:27

There is no happiness in wickedness. There is no happiness in doing the wrong thing of any kind. Joy comes of service. Joy comes of growth and activity in the ways of the Lord. I urge upon you the great importance of moving forward, having ever before you the example of the Savior of all mankind, even Jesus Christ. Pray in His name every night. Pray in His name every morning; and during the day exemplify in all of your activities the great virtues which He taught. I do not hesitate to promise you that if you do this, you will be happy and your lives will be productive.

BUSILY ENGAGED IN THE WORK

Behold, I say unto you that it is my will
that you should go forth and not tarry,
neither be idle but labor with your might.

—DOCTRINE AND COVENANTS 75:3

No man or woman will grow in this Church unless he or she carries a Church responsibility.

INDIVIDUAL EXCELLENCE

Remember the worth of souls is
great in the sight of God.

—DOCTRINE AND COVENANTS 18:10

You can be excellent in every way. You can be first class. There is no need for you to be a scrub. Respect yourself. Do not feel sorry for yourself. Do not dwell on unkind things others may say about you. Polish and refine whatever talents the Lord has given you. Go forward in life with a twinkle in your eye and a smile on your face, with great and strong purpose in your heart. Love life and look for its opportunities, and forever and always be loyal to the Church.

The Way to Peace and Happiness

And ye must practise virtue and
holiness before me continually.

—DOCTRINE AND COVENANTS 46:33

Believe in virtue! It is the only way to happiness! It is the only way to peace in one's heart. It is the only way of feeling right before the Lord and before one another.

FINANCIAL FREEDOM

Lay not up for yourselves treasures upon earth,
where moth and rust doth corrupt, and where
thieves break through and steal: But lay up for
yourselves treasures in heaven, where neither moth
nor rust doth corrupt, and where thieves do not
break through nor steal: For where your treasure
is, there will your heart be also.

—MATTHEW 6:19–21

We must be wise and frugal and careful and live within our means. Let us live within our means and get rid of debt. Some of it may be necessary. For education, for homes, yes. But for a fancy new car or a boat, no. The way to happiness is to be free, and one of the great freedoms is freedom from debt.

THANK THE LORD AND OFFER SACRIFICE

Thou shalt thank the Lord thy God in all things.
Thou shalt offer a sacrifice unto the Lord thy
God in righteousness, even that of a
broken heart and a contrite spirit.

—DOCTRINE AND COVENANTS 59:7–8

Before you make a decision against a mission, count your blessings, my dear friend. Think of all the great and marvelous blessings you have. Are they not all gifts from a generous Heavenly Father? Out of a spirit of appreciation and gratitude, and a sense of duty, you ought to make whatever adjustment is necessary to give a little of your time, consecrating your strength, your means, your talents to the work of sharing with others the gospel, which is the source of so much of the good that you have.

USING TIME WISELY

*For behold, this life is the time for men to prepare to
meet God; yea, behold the day of this life is the
day for men to perform their labors.*

—ALMA 34:32

Time is really all we have. And every individual
has an equal portion of it. The trick is to get more
out of what is available to us.

The Wisdom of the Ages

Whatever principle of intelligence we attain unto in this life, it will rise with us in the resurrection.

—DOCTRINE AND COVENANTS 130:18

I love libraries. I love books. There is something sacred, I think, about a great library because it represents the preservation of the wisdom, the learning, the pondering, of men and women of all of the ages accumulated together under one roof to which we can have access as our needs require.

Nurture the Individual

And if it so be that you should labor all your days
in crying repentance unto this people, and bring,
save it be one soul unto me, how great shall be your
joy with him in the kingdom of my Father!

—DOCTRINE AND COVENANTS 18:15

We are becoming a great global society. But our interest and concern must always be with the individual. Every member of this church is an individual man or woman, boy or girl. Our great responsibility is to see that each is remembered and nourished by the good word of God (see Moroni 6:4).... The organization can grow and multiply in numbers, as it surely will. But with all of this growth we must continue to nurture individuals. Jesus was the true shepherd who reached out to those in distress, one at a time, bestowing an individual blessing on each one. We must do the same.

LIVE IN, NOT OF, THE WORLD

And verily I say unto thee that thou shalt lay
aside the things of this world, and seek
for the things of a better.

—DOCTRINE AND COVENANTS 25:10

All of us live in the world. We cannot live a cloistered life. But we can live in the world without partaking of the unseemly ways of the world.

TRIUMPH OVER EVIL

For I the Lord cannot look upon sin with the least
degree of allowance; Nevertheless, he that
repents and does the commandments of
the Lord shall be forgiven.

—DOCTRINE AND COVENANTS 1:31–32

You can put behind you any evil with which you have been involved. The Lord has set up the machinery of repentance and forgiveness with helpful Church leaders to assist you in your difficulty. You can go forward with a renewal of hope and acceptability to a far better way of life.

TEACH FROM THE SCRIPTURES

And I give unto you a commandment
that you shall teach one another
the doctrine of the kingdom.

—DOCTRINE AND COVENANTS 88:77

Teach out of the word of God the doctrines of the kingdom which will save us and bless us and lift us.

THE GOSPEL OF GOOD NEWS

In me ye might have peace. In the world ye shall
have tribulation: but be of good cheer;
I have overcome the world.

—JOHN 16:33

Don't be gloomy. Even if you are not happy, put a smile on your face. This is the gospel of good news, this is a message of joy, this is the thing of which the angels sang when they sang at the birth of the Son of God. This is a work at eternal salvation; this is something to be happy and excited about.

THE STRENGTH OF CONVERTS

It was meet that we should make merry, and be
glad: for this thy brother was dead, and is
alive again; and was lost, and is found.

—LUKE 15:32

Every time a new member comes into the Church, something happens. There is an infusion of strength and faith and testimony that is wonderful.

DECLARATION OF BELIEF

And he said, Lord, I believe.

—JOHN 9:38

B e not afraid, only believe" (Mark 5:36). I commend these wonderful words to all who are called upon to stand up for what they believe, and to do so with confidence.

OVERLOOK WEAKNESS

Nevertheless let every one of you in particular so love his wife even as himself; and the wife see that she reverence her husband.

—EPHESIANS 5:33

Happiness in marriage involves a willingness to overlook weaknesses and mistakes.

THE STRENGTH OF TESTIMONIES

Behold, he changed their hearts; yea, he awakened them out of a deep sleep, and they awoke unto God.

—ALMA 5:7

What a marvelous and wonderful thing is this powerful conviction that says the Church is true. It is God's holy work. He overrules in the things of His kingdom and in the lives of His sons and daughters. The strength of this cause and kingdom is not found in its temporal assets, impressive as they may be. It is found in the hearts of its people. It comes of the gift of faith, bestowed by the Almighty upon His children who doubt not and fear not, but go forward.

REACH FOR YOUR TRUE POTENTIAL

*And God is able to make all grace abound toward
you; that ye, always having all sufficiency in all
things, may abound to every good work.*

—2 CORINTHIANS 9:8

You can and must rise above mediocrity, above
indifference.

REARING CHILDREN

But I have commanded you to bring up
your children in light and truth.

—DOCTRINE AND COVENANTS 93:40

Rear your children in love, in the nurture and admonition of the Lord. Take care of your little ones, welcome them into your homes, and love them with all of your hearts. They may do, in the years that come, some things you would not want them to do, but be patient, be patient. You have not failed as long as you have tried. Never forget that.

THE CONQUEST OF SELF

He that is slow to anger is better than the mighty;
and he that ruleth his spirit than
he that taketh a city.

—PROVERBS 16:32

The only conquest that brings satisfaction is the conquest of self. It was said of old that he who governs himself is greater than he who takes a city.

The Light of Knowledge

The glory of God is intelligence, or,
in other words, light and truth.

—DOCTRINE AND COVENANTS 93:36

In this world there are many who are unable to read or write. For them there is little light of ages past, and only diminished knowledge of the vast and intriguing world of the present. The darkness that surrounds them, the bleak shadow of illiteracy, condemns them to poverty, hunger, and ignorance. Do whatever you can to help them, whether they be in your home, neighborhood, or across the world. Bring light into their lives by helping them learn to read.

BE A RIGHTEOUS EXAMPLE

Ye are my disciples; and ye are a light unto this people, who are a remnant of the house of Joseph.

—3 NEPHI 15:12

More religion is caught than taught. Righteous living is a contagious thing. Teach by example. Be an example to others of one who walks the path of faith.

SELFLESS LABOR

*How beautiful upon the mountains are the feet of
him that bringeth good tidings, that publisheth
peace; that bringeth good tidings of good, that
publisheth salvation; that saith unto
Zion, Thy God reigneth!*

—ISAIAH 52:7

Every man or woman who goes forth in missionary service blesses the lives of all he or she teaches. Furthermore, his or her own life is enriched by this selfless labor.

NOVEMBER

*It is a good thing to give
thanks unto the Lord,
and to sing praises
unto thy name.*

—PSALM 92:1

LIVE EXEMPLARY LIVES

And let us not be weary in well doing: for in due season we shall reap, if we faint not. As we have therefore opportunity, let us do good unto all men.

—1 GALATIANS 6:9–10

Let us stand tall my brothers and sisters, as members of The Church of Jesus Christ of Latter-day Saints. Let us live exemplary lives. Let others see in us the kind of virtue that they would like to have come into their own lives. If we so live, God will bless us. We shall be His children, and He will be our Father, and we shall walk under His divine guidance in those paths which lead to immortality and eternal life.

THE SPIRIT OF THE TEMPLE

And many people shall go and say, Come ye, and let us go up to the mountain of the Lord, to the house of the God of Jacob; and he will teach us of his ways, and we will walk in his paths: for out of Zion shall go forth the law, and the word of the Lord from Jerusalem.

—ISAIAH 2:3

There is a need for constant improvement in all of our lives. There is a need occasionally to leave the noise and the tumult of the world and step within the walls of a sacred house of God, there to feel His spirit in an environment of holiness and peace.

RISE ABOVE CRITICISM

Thou shalt not speak evil of thy neighbor,
nor do him any harm.

—DOCTRINE AND COVENANTS 42:27

As a church, we are not without critics, some of whom are mean and vicious. We have always had them, and I suppose we will have them all through the future. But we shall go forward, returning good for evil, being helpful and kind and generous. Let us be good people. Let us be friendly people. Let us be neighborly people. Let us be what members of The Church of Jesus Christ of Latter-day Saints ought to be.

INVITATION TO PRAYER

*Pray always, that ye may not
faint, until I come.*

—DOCTRINE AND COVENANTS 88:126

Come to know our Father in Heaven. Say your prayers. Get on your knees and pray to the God of Heaven, and He will hear and answer your prayers.

READ THE BOOK OF MORMON

Verily, verily, I say unto you, I will impart unto you
of my Spirit, which shall enlighten your mind,
which shall fill your soul with joy.

—DOCTRINE AND COVENANTS 11:13

Without reservation I promise you that if you will prayerfully read the Book of Mormon, regardless of how many times you previously have read it, there will come into your hearts an added measure of the Spirit of the Lord. There will come a strengthened resolution to walk in obedience to His commandments, and there will come a stronger testimony of the living reality of the Son of God.

DON'T QUIT

And now, my beloved son, notwithstanding their
hardness, let us labor diligently; for if we should
cease to labor, we should be brought under
condemnation; for we have a labor to perform
whilst in this tabernacle of clay, that we may
conquer the enemy of all righteousness,
and rest our souls in the kingdom of God.

—MORONI 9:6

You have not failed until you quit trying.

RESPONSIBILITY OF
LATTER-DAY SAINTS

For unto whomsoever much is given,
of him shall be much required.

—LUKE 12:48

We have laid upon us as a people a greater charge, a greater responsibility than any other people have ever had in the history of the world. We are responsible for the blessings of the gospel of Jesus Christ to all who have lived upon the earth, to all who now live upon the earth, and to all who will yet live upon the earth. No other people have had so great a responsibility as that. God bless the faithful Latter-day Saints who carry in their hearts the love and respect of the great doctrine of the eternity of the family, and the tremendous doctrine of vicarious work for the dead.

BELIEVE IN YOURSELF

Cast not away therefore your confidence,
which hath great recompence of reward.

—HEBREWS 10:35

Believe in yourself. Believe in yourself as a child of God. Believe in your capacity to do good in the world, to spread light and truth and understanding; to reach out to those in distress and need to help and bless them.

LIVE VIRTUOUSLY

Who shall ascend into the hill of the Lord? or who
shall stand in his holy place? He that hath clean
hands, and a pure heart; who hath not lifted up
his soul unto vanity, nor sworn deceitfully.

—PSALM 24:3–4

There is nothing in all this world as magnificent as virtue. It glows without tarnish. It is precious and beautiful. It is above price. It cannot be bought or sold. It is the fruit of self-mastery. It comes with a promise of marvelous and wonderful blessings. He has said to those who live with virtue: "Then shall thy confidence wax strong in the presence of God. . . . The Holy Ghost shall be thy constant companion, and thy scepter an unchanging scepter of righteousness and truth; and thy dominion shall be an everlasting dominion" (D&C 121:45–46).

REACH BEYOND YOURSELF

And also, ye yourselves will succor those that stand
in need of your succor; ye will administer of your
substance unto him that standeth in need; and ye
will not suffer that the beggar putteth up his
petition to you in vain, and turn him out to perish.

—MOSIAH 4:16

The Savior was asked what is the greatest of the commandments. He replied, "Thou shalt love the Lord thy God with all thy heart, and with all thy soul, and with all thy mind. . . . And the second is like unto it, Thou shalt love thy neighbor as thyself" (Matthew 22:37–39). Every man and woman has the capacity to do great and good and wonderful things. We have an obligation to reach out beyond ourselves to help those in distress and trouble and difficulty wherever they may be, be they members of the Church or not.

THE PRINCIPLE OF SELF-RELIANCE

Prepare ye, prepare ye for that which is to come.

—DOCTRINE AND COVENANTS 1:12

Self-reliance is a principle of life. We ought to provide for ourselves and take care of our own needs. I encourage you to have something set aside, to plan ahead, to keep a little food on hand, to establish a savings account, if possible, against a rainy day. Catastrophes come to people sometimes when least expected—unemployment, sickness, things of that kind. The individual ought to do for himself all that he can. Only when he has exhausted his resources should he look to others and to the Church.

A SPIRIT OF THANKSGIVING

*Behold, my beloved brethren, remember the words
of your God; pray unto him continually by day,
and give thanks unto his holy name by
night. Let your hearts rejoice.*

—2 NEPHI 9:52

Let a spirit of thanksgiving guide and bless your days and nights.

DEVELOP CHARITY

But charity is the pure love of Christ, and it
endureth forever; and whoso is found possessed of it
at the last day, it shall be well with him.

—MORONI 7:47

Take the time to make the effort to care for others. Develop and exercise the one quality that would enable us to change the lives of others— what the scriptures call charity.

MISSIONARIES TEACH BY FAITH

*Ye have not chosen me, but I have chosen you, and
ordained you, that ye should go and bring forth
fruit, and that your fruit should remain: that
whatsoever ye shall ask of the Father in
my name, he may give it you.*

—JOHN 15:16

Missionaries go by the power of faith. Thousands of bright and able young men and women forgo social life, leave school, and selflessly go wherever they are sent to teach the gospel. They teach by the power of faith, planting a seed of faith here and another there which grows and matures into converts of strength and capacity.

GREED: AN INSIDIOUS TRAP

And he said unto them, Take heed, and beware of
covetousness: for a man's life consisteth not in the
abundance of the things which he possesseth.

—LUKE 12:15

Everyone wants to be successful. The question is: Successful at what? Successful at earning money, successful in marriage, successful in our own sight and in the eyes of our friends? None of these aspirations is necessarily wrong. But greed is an insidious trap that has the power to destroy those whose eager search for success becomes the driving force of their lives. Greed is the devious, sinister, evil influence that makes people say, "What I have is not enough. I must have more. And I will do whatever it takes to get it."

AVOID PORNOGRAPHY

Therefore remove sorrow from thy heart,
and put away evil from thy flesh.

—ECCLESIASTES 11:10

Not one of us can afford to partake of pornography. We cannot risk the damage it does to the most precious relationships—marriage—and to other interactions within the family. We cannot risk the effect it will have on our spirit and soul.

RIGHT AND WRONG

For do I now persuade men, or God? or do I seek to
please men? for if I yet pleased men, I should
not be the servant of Christ.

—GALATIANS 1:10

The kingdom of God is not a democracy. Wickedness and righteousness are not legislated by majority vote. Right and wrong are not determined by polls or pundits, though many would have us believe otherwise. Evil never was happiness. Happiness lies in the power and the sweet simplicity of virtue.

CHOOSE FRIENDS CAREFULLY

But I have prayed for thee, that thy faith fail not:
and when thou art converted,
strengthen thy brethren.

—LUKE 22:32

Everybody wants friends. Everybody needs friends. No one wishes to be without them. But never lose sight of the fact that it is your friends who will lead you along the paths that you will follow. While you should be friendly with all people, select with great care those whom you wish to have close to you. They will be your safeguards in situations where you may vacillate between choices, and you in turn may save them.

A THANKFUL HEART

And in nothing doth man offend God, or against
none is his wrath kindled, save those who
confess not his hand in all things.

—DOCTRINE AND COVENANTS 59:21

The habit of saying thank you is the mark of an educated man or woman. Express appreciation to everyone who does you a favor or assists you in any way. Thank the Lord for His goodness to you. Thank the Almighty for His Beloved Son, Jesus Christ, who has done for you what none other in all this world could do. Thank Him for His great example, for His tremendous teachings, for His outreaching hand to lift and help. Thank Him for His marvelous atonement. Confess His hand in all things.

RIGHTEOUS FATHERS

Hear, ye children, the instruction of a father.

—PROVERBS 4:1

Fathers have the basic and inescapable responsibility to stand as head of the family. That does not carry with it any implication of dictatorship or unrighteous dominion. It confers the mandate to provide for the needs of their families. Those needs are more than food, clothing, and shelter. Those needs include righteous direction and the teaching, by example as well as precept, of basic principles of honesty, integrity, service, respect for the rights of others, and an understanding that we are accountable, not only to one another but also to God, for that which we do in this life.

THE ROOT OF ALL EVIL

For what is a man profited, if he shall gain the whole world, and lose his own soul? or what shall a man give in exchange for his soul?

—MATTHEW 16:26

For the love of money is the root of all evil" (1 Timothy 6:10). That's true. When your mind is on the things of the world, you lose the Spirit of the Lord in your work. It isn't money that the Lord is talking about. It's the love of money. It's the covetousness, it's the greed, it's the desire to have more than you need which becomes the root of all evil.

HUNGER FOR THE WORD OF GOD

Blessed are they which do hunger and thirst after righteousness: for they shall be filled.

—MATTHEW 5:6

There is hunger in the land, and a genuine thirst—a great hunger for the word of the Lord and an unsatisfied thirst for things of the Spirit. I make a plea that we constantly seek the inspiration of the Lord and the companionship of his Holy Spirit to bless us in keeping our efforts on a high spiritual plane.

A TOUCH OF HUMOR

A merry heart maketh a cheerful countenance.

—PROVERBS 15:13

We need to have a little humor in our lives. We better take seriously that which should be taken seriously, but at the same time we can bring in a touch of humor now and again. If the time ever comes when we can't smile at ourselves, it will be a sad time.

JOY IN THE YOUTH

Rejoice, O young man, in thy youth; and let thy
heart cheer thee in the days of thy youth.

—ECCLESIASTES 11:9

I have great confidence in our young people as a whole. I regard you as the finest generation in the history of the church. I compliment you, and I have in my heart a feeling of love and respect and appreciation for you.

THE CUSTODIAL ROLE OF PARENTS

And all thy children shall be taught of the Lord;
and great shall be the peace of thy children.

—ISAIAH 54:13

Never forget that these little ones are the sons and daughters of God and that yours is a custodial relationship to them, that He was a parent before you were parents and that He has not relinquished His parental rights or interest in these His little ones.

A WORK OF LOVE

And this commandment have we from him,
That he who loveth God love his brother also.

—1 JOHN 4:21

Missionary work is a work of love and trust,
and it has to be done on that basis.

THE LONELINESS OF LEADERSHIP

And about the ninth hour Jesus cried with a loud
voice, saying, Eli, Eli, lama sabachthani? that is to
say, My God, my God, why hast thou forsaken me?

—MATTHEW 27:46

There is loneliness in all aspects of leadership. It was ever thus. The price of leadership is loneliness. The price of adherence to conscience is loneliness. But men and women of integrity must live with their convictions. Unless they do so, they are miserable—dreadfully miserable. I think it is inescapable. There is no lonelier picture in history than that of the Savior upon the cross, alone, the Redeemer of mankind, the Savior of the world, the Son of God suffering for the sins of all of us.

GIVE THANKS

*Live in thanksgiving daily, for the many mercies
and blessings which he doth bestow upon you.*

—ALMA 34:38

How magnificently we are blessed! How thankful we ought to be! Cultivate the spirit of thanksgiving in your lives. Make it of the very nature of your lives. It will impart an added dimension to your character that will give depth and strength.

THE QUEST FOR PERFECTION

And if men come unto me I will show unto them
their weakness. I give unto men weakness that they
may be humble; and my grace is sufficient for all
men that humble themselves before me; for . . . then
will I make weak things become strong unto them.

—ETHER 12:27

None of us will become perfect in a day or a month or a year. We will not accomplish it in a lifetime, but we can begin now, starting with our more obvious weaknesses and gradually converting them to strengths. This quest may be a long one; in fact, will be lifelong. It may be fraught with many mistakes, with falling down and getting back up again. But we must not sell ourselves short. We must make a little extra effort. Kneel before God in supplication. He will comfort, sustain, and bless us.

OUR CHILDREN'S WELL-BEING

We talk of Christ, we rejoice in Christ, we preach of
Christ . . . that our children may know to what
source they may look for a remission of their sins.

—2 NEPHI 25:26

It is not enough simply for parents to provide food and shelter for their children's physical well-being. There is an equal responsibility to provide nourishment and direction to the spirit and the mind and the heart.

DECEMBER

Verily I say unto you,
yea, and all the prophets
from Samuel and those
that follow after, as many
as have spoken, have
testified of me.

—3 NEPHI 20:24

THE HEALING POWER OF CHRIST

*Give to him that asketh thee, and from him that
would borrow of thee turn not thou away.*

—MATTHEW 5:42

Invite the healing power of Christ.

Jesus said: "I say unto you, That ye resist not
evil: but whosoever shall smite thee on thy right
cheek, turn to him the other also.... And whosoever
shall compel thee to go a mile, go with him twain"
(Matthew 5:39–41).

The application of this principle, difficult to
live but wondrous in its curative powers, would
have a miraculous effect on our troubled homes.
It is selfishness that is the cause of most of our
misery. It is as a cankering disease. The healing
power of Christ, found in the doctrine of going the
second mile, would do wonders to still argument
and accusation, fault-finding and evil speaking.

GRATITUDE FOR THE SEASON

Glory to God in the highest,
and on earth peace,
good will toward men.

—LUKE 2:14

I am grateful for Christmas. I am grateful for the spirit of the day and grateful for the outreach that comes into our hearts at this season of the year when we think a little more kindly of one another, when there is a little less of bitterness, when there is a little less of hate, when there is more of love and more of a reaching out to those in trouble and need and distress. I thank the Lord for Christmas.

CHARACTERISTICS OF GOD'S CHILDREN

He hath shewed thee, O man, what is good; and
what doth the Lord require of thee, but to
do justly, and to love mercy, and to
walk humbly with thy God?

—MICAH 6:8

We are sons and daughters of God, and it becomes us to live with respect toward one another—with integrity, with goodness in our lives, with honesty and uprightness before the Lord.

THE PRIVILEGE OF PRAYER

Evening, and morning, and at noon, will I pray,
and cry aloud: and he shall hear my voice.

—PSALM 55:17

I believe in prayer, the precious and wonderful privilege given each of us for our individual guidance, comfort, and peace.

LEARN OF CHRIST THROUGH THE SCRIPTURES

*Learn of me, and listen to my words; walk in
the meekness of my Spirit, and you
shall have peace in me.*

—DOCTRINE AND COVENANTS 19:23

We need to read the scriptures more. We need
to read the New Testament and renew our knowledge of the birth and life and ministry, the death
and the resurrection of Jesus. Each is a part of the
same picture. Had there been no resurrection there
likely would not be any remembrance of the birth.
They all go together in one great life: Jesus Christ,
the most perfect man who ever walked the earth.
We ought to get to know Him better. We would
have more of the spirit of Christmas, more of an
outreach to others, more concern for our neighbors, if we would do it.

THE GIFT OF ETERNAL LIFE

He shall come forth, and be born of a woman,
and he shall redeem all mankind
who believe on his name.

—ALMA 19:13

We honor the Beloved Son of our Eternal Father. It was Jesus, His firstborn, who left the glory of His Father's presence and condescended to come to earth as the promised Messiah. He has done for us what we could not do for ourselves. He has brought meaning to our mortal existence. He has given us the gift of eternal life. He was and is the Son of God.

READ THE WORDS OF CHRIST

My soul delighteth in the scriptures,
and my heart pondereth them.

—2 NEPHI 4:15

Read about Jesus Christ. Read His words in the New Testament and in Third Nephi in the Book of Mormon. Read them quietly to yourself and then ponder them. Pour out your heart to your Father in Heaven in gratitude for the gift of His Beloved Son.

DO NOT DESPAIR

All these things shall give thee experience,
and shall be for thy good.

—DOCTRINE AND COVENANTS 122:7

We are in a period of stress across the world. There are occasionally hard days for each of us. Do not despair. Do not give up. Look for the sunlight through the clouds. Opportunities will eventually open to you. Do not let the prophets of gloom endanger your possibilities.

GOD IS LOVE

And walk in love, as Christ also hath loved us.

—EPHESIANS 5:2

The Master taught: "For whosoever will save his life shall lose it: but whosoever will lose his life for my sake, the same shall save it" (Luke 9:24). This remarkable and miraculous process occurs in our own lives as we reach out with charity to serve others. Each of us can, with effort, successfully root the virtue of love deep in our beings so that we may be nourished by its great power all of our lives. For it is as we tap into the power of love that we come to understand the great truth written by John: "God is love; and he that dwelleth in love dwelleth in God" (1 John 4:16).

A SACRED TRUST

Finally, brethren, whatsoever things are true,
whatsoever things are honest, whatsoever things are
just, whatsoever things are pure, whatsoever things
are lovely, whatsoever things are of good report;
if there be any virtue, and if there be any
praise, think on these things.

—PHILIPPIANS 4:8

We cannot be less than honest, we cannot be less than true, we cannot be less than virtuous if we are to keep sacred the trust given us by those who have gone before us, or if we are to merit the trust and confidence of those with whom we live, work, and associate. Once it was said among our people that a man's word was as good as his bond. Shall any of us be less reliable, less honest than our fore-bears? Those who are dishonest with others canker their own souls and soon learn that they cannot trust even themselves.

VIRTUOUS LIVING

And let every man . . . practise virtue
and holiness before me.

—DOCTRINE AND COVENANTS 38:24

It all begins with our own personal virtue. Reformation of the world begins with reformation of self. We cannot hope to influence others in the direction of moral virtue unless we live lives of virtue. The example of our virtuous living will carry a greater influence than will all the preaching, postulating, and theorizing in which we might indulge. We cannot expect to lift others unless we are standing on higher ground.

WALK IN HUMILITY AND PRAYER

*Be thou humble; and the Lord thy God shall
lead thee by the hand, and give thee
answer to thy prayers.*

—DOCTRINE AND COVENANTS 112:10

There is no place for arrogance in our lives, no place for conceit, no place for anything of that kind. We are very ordinary people in many respects. We must walk our own way. We are here to do a work, to make something of our lives, and God our Eternal Father will bless us in so doing if we will walk in humility and prayer.

THE WINDOWS OF HEAVEN

Bring ye all the tithes into the storehouse, that there
may be meat in my house; and prove me now
herewith, saith the Lord of Hosts, if I will not
open you the windows of heaven, and pour
you out a blessing that there shall not
be room enough to receive it.

—3 NEPHI 24:10

The Lord will open the windows of heaven according to our need, and not according to our greed. If we are paying tithing to get rich, we are doing it for the wrong reason. The basic purpose for tithing is to provide the Church with the means needed to carry on His work. The blessing to the giver is an ancillary return and that blessing may not be always in the form of financial or material benefit. There are many ways in which the Lord can bless us beyond the riches of the world.

THE PURPOSE OF MORTALITY

If he shall be diligent in keeping my
commandments he shall be
blessed unto eternal life.

—DOCTRINE AND COVENANTS 18:8

The Lord did not send you here to fail. He did not give you life to waste it. He bestowed upon you the gift of mortality that you might gain experience—positive, wonderful, purposeful experience—that will lead to life eternal.

A POSITIVE ATTITUDE

Serve the Lord with gladness: come before his presence with singing. . . . Enter into his gates with thanksgiving, and into his courts with praise: be thankful unto him, and bless his name.

—PSALM 100:2, 4

Do you feel gloomy? Lift your eyes. Stand on your feet. Say a few words of appreciation and love to the Lord. Be positive. I do not know how anybody who is a member of this Church can feel gloomy for very long. This is the day which has been spoken of by those who have gone before us. Let us live worthy of our birthright. Keep the faith. Nurture your testimonies. Walk in righteousness and the Lord will bless you and prosper you, and you will be a happy and wonderful people.

FOLLOWERS OF CHRIST

Have ye received his image in
your countenances?

—ALMA 5:14

Stand as followers of the Lord Jesus Christ. None of us will fully reach a stage where we can walk as He walked in this life, but we can work at it. And the more we work at it, the more easily we shall take on the luster of His image in our own lives.

JESUS CHRIST IS HEAD OF THE CHURCH

To him give all the prophets witness, that through his name whosoever believeth in him shall receive remission of sins.

—ACTS 10:43

The Lord Jesus Christ is the head of this Church. He is its living head. The mission of the president of the Church, my chief responsibility, my greatest honor comes in bearing solemn testimony of His living reality.

THE MEANING OF CHRISTMAS

Thanks be unto God for his unspeakable gift.

—2 CORINTHIANS 9:15

Christmas means giving. The Father gave His Son, and the Son gave His life. Without giving there is no true Christmas, without sacrifice there is no true worship.

THE EFFECT OF CHRIST
ON HUMANKIND

Turn unto the Lord your God:
for he is gracious and merciful,
slow to anger, and of great kindness.

—JOEL 2:13

Brutality reigns where Christ is banished. Kindness and forbearance govern where Christ is recognized and His teachings are followed.

THE SPIRIT OF LOVE

It is the love of God, which sheddeth itself abroad
in the hearts of the children of men; wherefore,
it is the most desirable above all things.

—1 NEPHI 11:22

Christmas is more than trees and twinkling lights, more than toys and gifts and baubles of a hundred varieties. It is love. It is the love of the Son of God for all mankind. It reaches out beyond our power to comprehend. It is magnificent and beautiful.

REST ON THE SABBATH

Verily my sabbaths ye shall keep: for it is a sign between me and you throughout your generations.

—EXODUS 31:13

The Sabbath is such a precious thing. It represents the great culmination of the work of Jehovah in the creation of the earth and all that is found therein. When that was completed He looked upon it and saw that it was good and He rested on the Sabbath day. Now, I make a plea to our people to refrain from shopping on Sunday. You may say, "The little bit that I do doesn't make a bit of difference." It makes all the difference in the world to you and your children who will see your example.

THE NATURE OF TEMPLES

Whatsoever you bind on earth, in my name and by
my word, saith the Lord, it shall be eternally
bound in the heavens.

—DOCTRINE AND COVENANTS 132: 46

Everything that occurs in the temple is uplifting and ennobling. It speaks of life here and life beyond the grave. It speaks of the importance of the individual as a child of God. It speaks of the importance of the family and the eternity of the marriage relationship.

THE PROPHET JOSEPH

Joseph Smith, the Prophet and Seer of the Lord,
has done more, save Jesus only, for the
salvation of men in this world, than
any other man that ever lived in it.

—DOCTRINE AND COVENANTS 135:3

I bear solemn testimony of the divinity of Joseph Smith's call, of the magnitude of his accomplishments, of the virtue of his life, and of the security of his place among the great and honored of the Almighty in all generations of time. We stand in reverence before him. He is the great prophet of this dispensation. Let us not forget him. God be thanked for the Prophet Joseph.

The Living Christ

And now, after the many testimonies which have
been given of him, this is the testimony, last of all,
which we give of him: That he lives!

—DOCTRINE AND COVENANTS 76:22

We speak unabashedly of the living reality of the Lord Jesus Christ. We declare without equivocation the fact of His great act of atonement for all mankind. It is the substance of our theology. It is the wellspring of our faith.

THE SON OF GOD

For unto us a child is born, unto us a son is given:
and the government shall be upon his shoulder:
and his name shall be called Wonderful,
Counsellor, The mighty God, The everlasting
Father, The Prince of Peace.

—ISAIAH 9:6

Jesus Christ is the Son of God, who condescended to come into this world of misery,
struggle, and pain to touch men's hearts for good,
to teach the way of eternal life, and to give Himself
as a sacrifice for the sins of mankind. How different, how empty our lives would be without Him.
How infinite is our opportunity for exaltation
made possible through His redeeming love.

HE ANSWERS PRAYERS

I know that God will give liberally to him that
asketh. . . . Therefore I will lift up my
voice unto thee.

—2 NEPHI 4:35

Get on your knees and thank God for His goodness to you and express unto Him the righteous desires of your hearts. He hears, He responds, He answers. Not always as we would wish He would answer, but there is no question in my mind that He answers.

AN ANCHOR TO THE SOUL

And now, behold, whosoever is of my church, and
endureth of my church to the end, him will I
establish upon my rock, and the gates of
hell shall not prevail against them.

—DOCTRINE AND COVENANTS 10:69

Cling to the Church. If you will do so it will
become as an anchor in the midst of a stormy sea.
It will be a light to your lives and a foundation
upon which to build them.

THE BLESSINGS OF WORK

The labour of the righteous tendeth to life.

—PROVERBS 10:16

Work is the miracle by which talent is brought to the surface and dreams become reality.

INDIVIDUAL DIFFERENCES IN MARRIAGE

Let the husband render unto the wife due
benevolence: and likewise also the
wife unto the husband.

—1 CORINTHIANS 7:3

In a marriage, each of us is an individual. Each of us is different. There must be respect for differences, and although it is important and necessary that both the husband and the wife work to ameliorate those differences, there must be some recognition that they exist and that they are not necessarily undesirable. In fact, the differences may make the companionship more interesting.

A GREAT DAY OF OPPORTUNITY

Take fast hold of instruction; let her not go:
keep her; for she is thy life.

—PROVERBS 4:13

This is the great day of opportunity for you young people, this marvelous time to be upon the earth. You stand at the summit of all the past ages. You are exposed to the learning of all who have walked the earth, that learning being distilled down into courses where you can acquire knowledge in a relatively short time, the knowledge that men stumbled over in learning through all of the centuries past. Don't sell yourselves short. Don't miss your great opportunity. Get at it, work at it, study hard. The Lord has laid upon you a mandate to acquire secular knowledge as well as spiritual knowledge. Take advantage of the opportunities that are yours.

Focus on the Present

And now, Israel, what doth the Lord thy God
require of thee, but to fear the Lord thy God,
to walk in all his ways, and to love him,
and to serve the Lord thy God with all
thy heart and with all thy soul.

—DEUTERONOMY 10:12

I don't worry too much about the future, and I don't worry very much about the past. The past is gone, and you can't change, you can't correct it. The future, you can anticipate, but you can't necessarily do very much about it. It is the present you have to deal with. Reach out for every good opportunity to do what you ought to do.